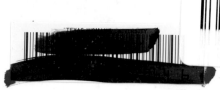
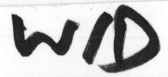

MORE
STAGE FAVOURITES OF THE
EIGHTEENTH CENTURY

" Yet, thus adorned with every graceful art
To charm the fancy, and to reach the heart."

"THE RIVALS"—*Sheridan*

MORE STAGE FAVOURITES
of the
EIGHTEENTH CENTURY

By
LEWIS S. BENJAMIN
(LEWIS MELVILLE , PSEUD.)

WITH A FRONTISPIECE BY LESLIE BLANCH
AND SIXTEEN OTHER ILLUSTRATIONS

Essay Index Reprint Series

BOOKS FOR LIBRARIES PRESS, INC.
FREEPORT, NEW YORK

First published 1929
Reprinted 1967

LIBRARY OF CONGRESS CATALOG NUMBER:

67-28743

TO
LEON M. LION

PREFACE

LAST year I published a volume called " Stage Favourites of the Eighteenth Century," in which I printed biographical studies of popular performers of the period in question :

Anne (" Nance ") Oldfield, 1683–1730 ;

Lavinia Fenton (*née* Beswick), afterwards Duchess of Bolton, 1708–1760 ;

Catherine (" Kitty ") Clive (*née* Raftor), 1711–1785 ;

Hannah Pritchard (*née* Vaughan), 1711–1768 ;

Charlotte Charke (*née* Cibber), died 1760 ;

Margaret (" Peg ") Woffington, 1714(?)–1760 ;

Susannah Maria Cibber (*née* Arne), 1714–1766 ; and

George Anne Bellamy, 1731(?)–1788.

It will be observed that the earliest of these ladies, Nance Oldfield, was born in 1683, and that the last to depart was George Anne Bellamy, who died in 1788.

In the present volume, of the four actresses, Frances Abington was born in 1737, and each of them survived until the nineteenth century, " Perdita " Robinson, the first to go, only just managing to survive until December 26, 1800.

It has been my object in these volumes rather to present character studies than to trace in detail the theatrical careers of the actresses whom I have taken as my subjects. Anything more dreary than long lists of parts in mostly forgotten plays it is difficult to conceive. Those who wish to supplement such information as I have given will be able to do so by consulting " Some Accounts of the English Stage from the Restoration in 1660 to 1832," by the Rev. John Genest, which was published in 1832 at Bath, in ten volumes, and is indubitably the standard authority on the matter.

For assistance in the preparation of these volumes, my thanks are due to Mrs. E. Constance Monfrino, Major Reginald Hargreaves, M.C., and Mr. Alfred Sydney Lewis, Librarian of the Constitutional Club.

LEWIS S. BENJAMIN
(LEWIS MELVILLE.)

LONDON,
May, 1929

CONTENTS

LIST OF ILLUSTRATIONS

FRANCES ABINGTON
(*née* BARTON)
1737–1815

FRANCES ABINGTON
(*née* BARTON)
1737–1815

"THE following 'Life of Mrs. Abington, formerly Miss Frances or Fanny Barton,' is sent forth in full confidence of a hearty welcome by the public. This celebrated lady achieved so high a position in the comic walks of theatrical life, and was so famed for her personal beauty and exquisite taste in those matters of dress which are so dear to the female heart, that anything like a consecutive narrative of her career must be of general interest." Thus an anonymous biographer, who is not in all matters to be relied upon.

Frances claimed—or, perhaps, when she became famous, it was claimed for her—that she was descended from a family that had already in the reign of William III attained distinction, the head of which at the time of the Revolution was Christopher Barton, of Norton, Derbyshire, who had four sons, one of whom entered the Army and rose to the rank of colonel; another became a Ranger of a royal park; another was "an ecclesiastic" of Westminster; and the fourth would appear to have been distinguished for nothing more than being the grandfather of Frances. There is, however, no doubt, that the family, or anyhow her branch of it, had fallen upon evil days, for when the actress was born her parents were in a very lowly condition. Her father, who had served as a private in the King's Guard, when off duty worked at a cobbler's stall in Windmill Street, Haymarket, and her brother was an ostler and watered the horses of the Hampstead stage-coach at the corner of Hanway Street, off Tottenham Court Road. Of her mother nothing is known, not even her name or the year of her death.

In the circumstances, Frances, from a very early age, had to do her best to help to support herself and her family. She has been described as "a vivacious and intelligent little girl, selling flowers in St. James's Park." She was then known as " Nosegay Fan," and her good looks as a child brought her many customers. She sang in the streets, and was occasionally permitted to sing in the better class of coffee-houses, such as the Bedford, and the Shakespeare in the Piazza, Covent Garden, when, according to one account, " to the company met in the private rooms of these establishments she would from a stage, extemporised from a table, recite various passages from the poets, her efforts and beauty winning the reward of a few pence from her auditors." Presently she became the servant of a French milliner in Cockspur Street, for whom she ran errands ; and then she was a cook-maid in the kitchen of Robert Baddeley. Then, says John Doran, " ensued some passages in her life that remind one of the training and experiences of Nell Gwyn. The

FRANCES ABINGTON AS MISS PRUE
After an engraving by Thornthwaite from a painting by J. Roberts

fascinating Fanny, in one way or another, made her way in the world, and, for the sake of a smile, lovers courted ruin. This excessively brilliant, though not edifying, career, did not last long." She was, however, evidently a girl with a personality and, unquestionably, even when quite youthful, with ambition. Though she did not know what was to be her career, she studied in her leisure, and acquainted herself with French and Italian, in both of which languages it is said that she could converse.

How, then, Frances Barton lived until she was eighteen is best left to the imagination. When she had attained that age she was so fortunate as to succeed in getting a footing on the stage. Theophilus (the reprobate son of Colley) Cibber had obtained a licence from the Lord Chamberlain to present plays for a certain number of nights at the theatre in the Haymarket. To him Frances applied successfully, and she was given her first chance as Miranda in *The Busy-Body* to his Marplot on August 21, 1755. Her abilities were evident, and she was allowed to gain further experience by appearing as Miss Jenny in *The Provoked Husband*, Kitty Pry in *The Lying Valet*, Sylvia in *The Recruiting Officer*, Prince Prettyman in *The Rehearsal*, and Mrs. Tattoo in *Lethe*. As a proof of her merits as an actress she was soon entrusted with the part of Desdemona. She was then engaged by Slater for the theatre at Bath, and there and at Richmond she played for a year, when Lacy, who had seen several of her performances, engaged her for Drury Lane. She made her first appearance at this

B

theatre on October 29, 1756, as Lady Pliant in *The Double Dealer*. In the strong cast were Henry Mossop, Samuel Foote, Henry Woodward, John Palmer, Hannah Pritchard, and Kitty Clive. Frances's name was not given, but her character was announced in the bills as being played by a " young gentlewoman appearing for the first time."

Frances Barton was soon established at Drury Lane, though the presence in the company of those experienced and popular actresses, Mrs. Pritchard, Maria Macklin, and Kitty Clive, for some time kept her out of the parts for which she was especially qualified. However, she was entrusted to create Arabella in Foote's *Cato ;* and she played, among many other parts, Mrs. Termagant in *The Squire of Alsatia*, Dorcas in *The Mock Doctor*, and Rodamintha in *Zara*, Lucy in *The Beggar's Opera*, and Maria in *Arden of Faversham*.

Frances, anxious to equip herself thoroughly, determined to study music, and she called in for her instructor one James Abington, described as " a trumpeter in the royal service." Him she married in or before September, 1759, after which her married name was given. According to one account, they set up " a splendid home in the then fashionable quarter of St. Martin's Lane," though as the husband was certainly not well off and the salary of the actress at this time was but thirty shillings a week, it would be interesting to know how the expenses were defrayed. " Soon afterwards," says Doran, "the convenient Apollo disappears, and even the musical dictionaries fail to tell us of the being and whereabouts of a man whose wife made his name famous." The marriage was from the first unhappy. A contemporary biographer writes : " As Mrs. Abington grew popular, her husband showed unmistakable signs of jealousy, whether justifiable or not it is not easy to say, but things came to such a pitch, and the dissatisfaction grew so mutual, that by common consent they parted. A regular agreement was some time after entered into, and she covenanted to pay him a certain sum per annum, on condition that he neither came near her nor in any way molested her. That he lived some years in the receipt of this pension is pretty generally believed ; but he soon disappeared from public notice, and was speedily forgotten."

At the end of 1759 Mrs. Abington severed, temporarily, her connection with Drury Lane. One reason undoubtedly was the fact that her promotion was barred by the claims of the older actresses. Another is given by Tate Wilkinson : " Mr. Garrick, not perceiving her merit, or in fear that encouragement would be for claiming advancement of terms, did not seem inclined to introduce her to advantage before the public ; but, my then intimate friend Mrs. Abington formed a better opinion of her own deserts, and, thinking Mr. Garrick intended injury, instead of acting friendly, she, without ceremony, suddenly eloped, in December, to her former manager and friend Mr. Anthony Brown."

The theatre in Smock Alley, Dublin, was in a most lamentable condition financially, but an effort was now being made to put it on its feet. " Mr. Brown," Wilkinson continues, " communicated with Mrs. Abington, and, so high was his opinion of her merit, that, without qualification, he offered the choice of every leading character whatever if she would quit her engagement at Drury Lane and join him in his venture. His offers were too tempting to an actress whose subordinate position rendered impossible a full development of her talents, and who was in the receipt of but thirty shillings a week, to be refused, she accepted his proposals and embarked for Ireland, where she arrived early in December."

Mrs. Abington made her first appearance in Dublin on December 11, 1759, as Mrs. Sullen in *The Stratagem*, and was at once successful. " Every night she appeared," says her earliest biographer, " she added to her reputation, and, before the season closed, notwithstanding every disadvantage, and many there were, particularly that of not having received the London stamp of fashion and approbation, she was considered as one of the first and most promising actresses on the stage. . . . Her acting, especially in certain pieces, fairly took the town by storm, and her taste in dress was regarded by the ladies of fashion as so good and correct that it became quite the rage to wear articles bearing her name. Her position was very different to what it had been when employed at Drury Lane ; leading, instead of subordinate and inferior, parts were now assigned to her, and the improvement in her earnings enabled her to make the arrangement alluded to, by which she relieved herself of the presence of her uncongenial husband."

John O'Keefe, in his *Recollections*, had much that was flattery to say of her : " Mrs. Abington's manner was charmingly fascinating, and her speaking voice melodious. She had peculiar tricks in acting, one was turning her wrist, and seeming to stick a pin in the side of her waist. She was also very adroit in the exercise of her fan ; and though equally capital in fine ladies and roydens, was never seen in low or vulgar characters. On her benefit night the pit was always railed into the boxes ; her acting shone brightest when doing Estefania to Brown's Copper Captain. This refers, of course, to the season 1759–60, when she was in Dublin, and before she received the stamp of a London audience.

" Her Kitty in *High Life below Stairs* created a sort of infatuation for her at the Smock Alley Theatre," Doran records. " Her name was, so to speak, on the public lip, and in ten days her cap was so much the fashion that there was not a milliner's shop but what was adorned by it, and ' Abington ' appeared in large letters to attract the passers-by." James Boaden, the biographer of Peg Woffington and Mrs. Siddons, also pays tribute to her : " Ireland, as a school for a young actress, had long been rendered of first-rate importance by the brilliant career of Mrs. Abington, who acted at both the Dublin theatres, and unquestionably showed very peculiar and unapproached talent. She, I think, took more entire possession of the stage than any actress I have ever seen. There was, however, no assumption in her dignity; she was a lawful and graceful sovereign, who exerted her full power and enjoyed her established prerogatives. The ladies of the day wore the hoop and its concomitants. The spectator's exercise of the fan was really no play of fancy. Shall I say that I have never seen it in a hand so dexterous as that of Mrs. Abington? She was a woman of great application; to speak as she did required more thought than usually attends female study, for the greater part of the sex rely upon an intention which seldom misleads them, such discernment as it gives becomes habitual, and is commonly sufficient, or sufficient for common purposes. But commonplace was not the station of Abington. She was always beyond the surface, untwisted all the chains that bind ideas together, and seized upon the exact cadence and emphasis by which the point of the dialogue is enforced. Her voice was of high pitch, and not very powerful. Her management of it alone made it an organ, yet this was so perfect that we sometimes converted the mere effect into a cause, and supposed it was the sharpness of the tone that had conveyed the sting. Yet, her figure considered, her voice sounded rather inadequate; its articulation, however, gave both strength and smartness to it, though it could not give sweetness. You heard her well, and without difficulty, and it is the first duty of a public speaker to be audible and intelligible. Her deportment is not so easily described; more womanly than Farren; fuller, yet not heavy, like Young; and far beyond even the conception of modern fine ladies. Mrs. Abington remains in memory as a thing for chance to restore us rather than design, and revive our polite comedy at the same time."

Let one more admirer speak. "From my dear Dublin and good friends," Tate Wilkinson writes, "I took my farewell early in March, 1760, and left Mrs. Abington at the pinnacle where she had many years sat smiling, and been looked at and admired with sincere pleasure and respect by the first persons in both the kingdoms."

To return to Mrs. Abington's private affairs. "Availing herself of the liberty afforded by the separation (from her husband), she appears to have regarded herself as a single woman again, and apparently was looked upon in the same light by others," her first biographer writes. "In order to rid herself of the crowd of admirers who daily surrounded her, and, emboldened by her husband's absence, did not scruple openly to declare their love, and to enjoy quiet under what she called an honourable protection (since the circumstances of her position prevented her accepting any proposals of marriage), she yielded at last to the solicitations of a gentleman of family, fortune, and learning, who had made the tour of Europe, and was Member of Parliament for Newry in the county of Down. This connection, brought about through an approving choice of the mind on both sides, rather than the gratification of any other wish, the pleasure arising from this intercourse became gradually so intense that he delighted in no

company so much as hers, each was a great and
irresistible attraction to the other, and while she
found herself unable to withdraw herself from his
company, he was charmed in cultivating a mind
happily disposed to receive and profit by his instruction, enjoying a singular satisfaction in reading,
explaining, and communicating to her every kind of
knowledge.

" Business calling this gentleman to England shortly
after, an opportunity was afforded Mrs. Abington of
revisiting her native country," the biographer continues. " The great reputation she had at once
achieved in Ireland had very speedily attracted the
attention of English managers, and Mr. Garrick had
thought it worth his while to make her what was then
considered an extravagant offer to return to Drury
Lane, an offer she declined accepting until Garrick
returned from Italy and re-occupied his own house.
Meanwhile, her protector's state of health became so
bad as to give rise to serious apprehension respecting
the future, and, impelled by a sense of duty and affection, she attended him to Bath and some other places
that it was hoped might assist in his recovery ; but
a constitutional malady, under which he had laboured
from his infancy, at last getting the better of him,
and threatening him with the approach of that final
tribute, he bethought himself seriously of leaving out
of the reach of adversity a faithful friend and companion who had devoted herself to him, and whose
behaviour during his last illness was such as the most
heroic matron might not be ashamed to copy.   His

heirs after discharged in a very honourable manner
the provision he had made for her, and she was also
favoured by the family with a notice that is rarely
the consequence of an attachment of such a nature."

Her lover being dead, Mrs. Abington at last yielded
to the pressing invitation of Garrick to join his company at Drury Lane. Her salary was fixed at five
pounds a week, which salary was not then thought
to be ungenerous. The difficulty of finding a good
part for her, however, seemed at first to present a
formidable obstacle to her occupancy at Drury Lane
of the position for which she was adapted. Nearly
all those in which she had been so successful in Dublin
were in the possession of Kitty Clive and Mrs. Pritchard, the Widow Belmour in Arthur Murphy's
comedy, *The Way to Keep Her*. In this part, on
November 27, 1765, she made her reappearance after
an absence of nearly six years. So admirable was her
performance, that years later when the author
reprinted another play, *The Way to Keep Him*, he
dedicated it to her.

Arthur Murphy to Mrs. Abington.

"LINCOLN'S INN,

"*November 25, 1785.*

"MADAM,

"You will be surprised at this distance of
time, and in this public manner, to receive an answer
to a very polite letter which you addressed to me in
the course of the last summer at Yarmouth. In a
strain of vivacity, which always belongs to you, you

invite me to write again for the stage. You will tell me that having gone through the comedies of *The Way to Keep Him*, *All in the Wrong*, and *Three Weeks after Marriage* you now want more from the same hand. I am not bound, you say, by my resolution, signified in a prologue about ten years ago, to take my leave of the dramatic muse. At the perjury of poets, as well as lovers, Jove laughs, and the public, you think, will be ready to give me a general release from the promise. All this is very flattering. If the following scenes, at the end of five-and-twenty years, still continue to be a part of the public amusement, I know to what cause to ascribe it. Those graces of action, with which you adorn whatever you undertake, have given to the piece a degree of brilliancy, and even novelty, as often as you have repeated it. I am not unmindful of the performers who first obtained for the author the favour of the town ; a Garrick, a Yates, a Cibber, united for abilities ; and who can forget Mrs. Clive ? They have all passed away, and the comedy might have passed with them if you had not so frequently placed it in a conspicuous light.

" The truth is, without such talents as yours, all that the poet writes is a dead letter—he designs for representation, but it is the performer who gives to the draught, however justly traced, a form, a spirit, a countenance, and a mind. All this you have done for the Widow Belmour ; and that excellence in your art, which you are known to possess, can, no doubt, lend the same animation to any new character. But, alas ! I have none to offer. That tinder in the poet's mind, which, as Doctor Young says, takes fire from every spark, I have not found, even though you have endeavoured to kindle the flame. Could I write as you can act, I should be proud to obey your commands ; but after a long disuse, how shall I recover the train of thinking necessary for plot, humour, incident, and character ?

" In the place of novelty, permit me to request that *The Way to Keep Him* may be inscribed to you. You are entitled to it, Madam, for your talents have made the play your own. A dedication, I grant, at this period of time, comes rather late ; but being called upon for a new edition, I have retouched the dialogue, and perhaps so reformed the whole that in its present state it may be deemed less unworthy of your acceptance. It is, therefore, my wish that this address may in future attend the comedy, to remain (as long as such a thing can remain) a tribute due to the genius of Mrs. Abington and a mark of that esteem with which I subscribe myself,

" Madam,

" Your real admirer

" And most obedient servant,

" ARTHUR MURPHY."

During the eighteen years from 1765 that she was at Drury Lane Mrs. Abington played a great number of parts. Amongst them were Lady Fanciful in *The Provoked Wife*, with Mrs. Cibber as Lady Brute and

Garrick as Sir John Brute ; Betty in *The Clandestine Marriage ;* Estefania in *Rule a Wife* (for her own benefit in 1766) ; Miss Lucy in *The Virgin Unmasked ;* Lucy in *The Beggar's Opera ;* Millamont in *The Way of the World ;* Lady Townly in *The Provoked Husband ;* and Mrs. Sullen in *The Stratagem.* Her principal Shakespearian characters were Ophelia, Portia, Beatrice, Desdemona, and Olivia.

Mrs. Abington created Lady Teazle in *The School for Scandal* in 1777 with great success. " To my great astonishment," Horace Walpole wrote on that occasion to Robert Jephson, " there were more parts performed admirably in *The School for Scandal* than I almost ever saw in any play. Mrs. Abington was equal to the first of her profession, Yates (the husband), William Parsons [the original Crabtree], Miss Pope, and John Palmer [the original Joseph Surface] all shone. It seemed a marvellous resurrection of the stage. Indeed, the play had as much merit as the actors. I have seen no comedy that comes near it since *The Provoked Husband.*" Walpole loved the actress personally, as his correspondence clearly indicates. There is an amusing passage in one of his letters to Conway, dated May 1779, written from his house at Arlington Street : " Adieu ! I am going to sup with Mrs. Abington, and hope that Mrs. Clive will not hear of it."

Horace Walpole to Frances Abington.

" Mr. Walpole cannot express how much he is mortified that he cannot accept of Mrs. Abington's

obliging invitation, as he had engaged company to
dine with him on Sunday at Strawberry Hill, whom
he would put of, if not foreigners who are leaving
England. Mr. Walpole hopes, however, that this
accident will not prevent an acquaintance which his
admiration of Mrs. Abington's genius has made him
long desire; and which he hopes to cultivate at
Strawberry Hill, when her leisure will give him leave
to trouble her with an invitation."

Horace Walpole to Frances Abington.

" Paris,

" *September* 1, 1771.

" If I had known, madam, of your being at Paris,
before I heard it from Colonel Blaquiere, I should
certainly have prevented your flattering invitation,
and have offered you any services that could depend
on my acquaintance here. It is plain I am old and
live with very old folks, when I did not hear of your
arrival. However, madam, I have not that fault at
least of a veteran, the thinking nothing equal to what
they admired in their youth. I do impartial justice
to your merit, and fairly allow it not only equal to
that of any actress I have seen, but believe the present
age will not be in the wrong, if they hereafter prefer
it to those they may live to see. Your allowing
me to wait on you in London, madam, will make
me some amends for the loss I have had
here."

Horace Walpole to Frances Abington.

" STRAWBERRY HILL,

" *June* 11, 1780.

" MADAM,

" You may certainly always command me and my house. My common custom is to give a ticket for only four persons at a time ; but it would be very insolent in me, when all laws are set at naught, to pretend to subscribe rules. At such times there is a shadow of authority in setting the law aside by the legislature itself ; and though I have no army to supply their place, I declare Mrs. Abington may march through all my dominions at the head of as large a troop as she pleases—I do not say, as she can muster and command, for then I am sure my house would not hold them. The day, too, is at her own choice, and the master is her very obedient servant,

" HOR. WALPOLE."

Evidently, as the years passed, Walpole altered his opinion of Mrs. Abington as an actress.

Horace Walpole to the Countess of Ossory.

" *June* 14, 1787.

" Who should act genteel comedy perfectly, but persons of fashion who have sense ? Actors and actresses can only guess at the tone of high life, and can *not* be inspired with it. Why are there so few genteel comedies, but because most comedies are written by men of that sphere ? Etheredge, Congreve,

Vanbrugh, and Cibber wrote genteel comedy, because they lived in the best company; and Mrs. Oldfield played it so well, because she not only followed, but often set, the fashion. General Burgoyne has written the best modern comedy for the same reason; and Miss Farren is as excellent as Mrs. Oldfield, because she has lived with the best style of men in England, whereas Mrs. Abington can never go beyond Lady Teazle, which is a second-rate character, and that rank of women are always aping women of fashion, without arriving at the style."

Dr. Johnson, too, liked her, if Boswell is to be believed. "On Monday, March 25, 1775, I breakfasted with Dr. Johnson at Mr. William Strahan's," he says. "He told us he was engaged to go that evening to Mrs. Abington's benefit: 'she was visiting some ladies whom I was visiting, and begged that I would come to her benefit. I told her I could not hear; but she insisted so much on my coming that it would have been brutal to have refused her.' This was a speech quite characteristical. He loved to bring forward his having been in the gay circles of life, and he was perhaps a little vain of the solicitations of this elegant and fashionable actress. He told us the play was to be *The Hypocrite*, altered from Cibber's *Nonjuror*, so as to satirise the Methodists."

Johnson cannot have enjoyed himself. "I met him at Drury Lane playhouse in the evening," Boswell relates. "Sir Joshua Reynolds, at Mrs. Abington's request, had promised to bring a body of wits to her

Benefit ; and having secured forty places in the front
boxes, had done me the honour to put me in the group.
Johnson sat in the seat directly behind me, and as
he could neither see nor hear at such a distance from
the stage he was wrapped up in grave abstraction,
and seemed quite a cloud amidst all the sunshine of
glitter and gaiety. I wondered at his patience in
sitting out a play of five acts and a farce or two. He
said very little ; but after the prologue to *Bon Ton*
[by Garrick] had been spoken, which he could hear
pretty well from the more slow and distinct utterance,
he talked of prologue writing, and observed, ' Dryden
has written prologues superior to any David Garrick
has written ; but David Garrick has written more
good prologues than Dryden has done. It is wonderful
that he has been able to write such variety of them.' "

Johnson later referred to that evening. Fanny
Burney has related how seven years later the Hon.
Mary Monckton (afterwards Countess of Cork) told
him that he must see Mrs. Siddons. " Well, Madam,"
he answered, " if you desire it I will go. See her I
shall not, nor hear her ; but I'll go, and that will do.
The last time I was at a play I was ordered there by
Mrs. Abington, or Mrs. Somebody, I do not well
remember who ; but I placed myself in the middle
of the first row of the front boxes to show that when
I was called I came."

" On Saturday, April 8, 1775," Boswell notes, " I
dined with Dr. Johnson at Mrs. Thrale's. Johnson
had supped the night before at Mrs. Abington's, with
some fashionable people whom he named ; and he

ELIZABETH FARREN, COUNTESS OF DERBY
After a portrait by Zoffany

seemed much pleased with having made one in so elegant a circle. Nor did he omit to pique his ' mistress ' (as he called Mrs. Thrale) a little with jealousy of her housewifery, for he said (with a smile), ' Mrs. Abington's jelly, my dear lady, was better than yours.' "

Though they acted long together, the relations between Mrs. Abington and David Garrick were not harmonious. That great authority on theatrical history, Dutton Cook, sums up the situation : " Garrick wrote of her, on the back of one of her letters, that she was ' the worst of women.' Of his merits as an actor she spoke enthusiastically ; but she pronounced him as a manager inconsiderate, harsh, and resentful. She maintained with him a long and acrimonious correspondence. He complained of her peevish letters, of her want of zeal for the interests of the theatre, of her incessant querulousness. She alleged that he caused her to be attacked in the newspapers, that his harshness affected her health and spirits, that he spoke ill of her wherever he went. Again and again she asked that her engagement might be cancelled, and that she might be released from the inconvenience and distress of her position at Drury Lane." Yet, in May 1774 she entered into an agreement with Garrick and Lacy to play at that theatre for three acting seasons at a salary of twelve pounds a week, with a benefit, and sixty pounds for clothes.

The correspondence is not without interest. At least it shows some of the troubles with which Garrick had to contend, and also that the actress was a very

c

difficult person with whom to work—" temperamental " she would be called to-day.

Frances Abington to William Hopkins.

Friday morning, Jan. 30, 1774.

" Mrs. Abington sent the part of Letitia in *The Choleric Man*, to Mr. Hopkins, in order to his receiving Mr. Garrick's command as to the person he is pleased to give it in study to, for the next representation of the play. Mr. Cumberland has obligingly given his consent to her resigning of the part ; and Mrs. Abington flatters herself that Mr. Garrick will have the goodness and complaisance to relieve her from a character so little calculated to her very confined style of acting. Mrs. Abington has been very ill for some days past, but would not importune Mr. Garrick with complaints, as she saw there was a necessity for exerting herself till the new tragedy was ready."

Frances Abington to David Garrick.

" *Wednesday morning*, 1774.

" Indeed, Sir, I could not play Violante to-morrow if my happiness in the next world depended upon it ; but if you order me, I will look it over, and be perfect as soon as possible. Mrs. Sullen is ready, and I am sure if you are pleased to give yourself a moment's time to reflect upon my general conduct in the theatre, you will see that I ever made my attention to my business and my duty to you my sole object and ambition."

Agreement with Mrs. Abington.

" *May* 5, 1774.

" It is agreed between Mrs. Abington and Mr. Garrick, that the former shall be engaged to him and Mr. Lacy, patentees of the Theatre Royal in Drury Lane, for three years from this date, of three acting seasons, at the sum of twelve pounds a week with a benefit, and sixty pounds for clothes, the above agreement to be put into article according to the usual form.

" FRANCES ABINGTON,

" D. GARRICK,

" For Mr. Lacy and himself."

MRS. ABINGTON HAS PLAYED THIS SEASON

Oct.	Sat.	7.	Way of the World.	
	Wed.	11.	Rule a Wife.	
	Fri.	20.	Stratagem.	
	Sat.	21.	Conscious Lovers.	Bon Ton.
	Mond.	23.	,, ,,	,,
	Tues.	24.	,, ,,	,,
	Thurs.	26.	,, ,,	,,
	Fri.	27.	Way of the World.	Bon Ton.
	Mond.	30.	Conscious Lovers.	
	Tues.	31.	Provoked Wife.	
Nov.	Wed.	1.	,,	,,
	Mond.	6.	Much Ado.	
	Wed.	8.	,,	
	Fri.	10.	,,	
	Tues.	14.	Much Ado.	,,
	Thurs.	16.	,,	
	Wed.	22.	,,	
	Tues.	28.	Maid of the Oaks.	
	Thurs.	30.	,, ,,	

Dec.	Fri.	1.	Stratagem.	
	Mond.	4.	Maid of the Oaks.	
	Tues.	5.	Rule a Wife.	
	Wed.	6.	Maid of the Oaks.	Bon Ton.
	Tues.	12.	,, ,,	Sultan
	Wed.	13.	,, ,,	,,
	Thurs.	14.	,, ,,	,,
	Fri.	15.	,, ,,	,,
	Wed.	20.	Rule a Wife.	,,
	Thurs.	21.	,,	..
	Sat.	23.	Stratagem.	
Jan.	Wed.	3.	Hypocrite.	
	Mond.	22.	Discovery.	
	Wed.	24.	,,	
	Fri.	26.	,,	
	Sat.	27.	,,	
	Mond.	29.	,,	
Feb.	Wed.	7.	,,	
	Thurs.	8.	Maid of the Oaks.	
	Sat.	10.	,, ,,	Bon Ton.
	Mond.	12.	Much Ado.	
	Wed.	14.	Rule a Wife.	Sultan.
	Mond.	19.	,,	,,

David Garrick to Frances Abington.

" ADELPHI,

" *Sept.* 26, 1774.

" As no business can be done without being explicit, I must desire to know if you choose to perform Mrs. Sullen [in *The Stratagem*]. The part is reserved for you, and the play must be acted soon : whoever does it with Mr. Smith must do it with me—supposing that I am ever able to be the rake again. We talked a great deal last night, and I am sorry to say it, without my having the least idea what to do in consequence of it. If *The Tender Husband* can be done with credit, I shall immediately set to work, and with *The Hypocrite*. I cannot create better actors than we have, and we must do our best with them. Could I put you upon the highest comic pinnacle, I certainly would do it ; but indeed, my dear Madam, we shall not mount much if your cold counteracting discourse is to pull us back at every step. Don't imagine that the gout makes me peevish ; I am talking to you in the greatest good humour ; but if we don't do our best with the best we have, it is all fruitless murmuring and inactive repining. Something too much of this. I shall write to the author of the piece to-morrow night, which I read to you. I have yet obeyed but half his commands, as he wrote the character of Lardoon [in *The Maid of the Oaks* by General Burgoyne] for your Ladyship. I must beg of you to speak your thoughts upon that, which after I have read it to you, I promised to let him know your sentiments. I could wish, if you say any thing to me of our stage business, you would send it separately from your opinion of *The Maid of the Oaks* and *Lady Bab :* with your leave I could wish to enclose what you say of the last of the author."

David Garrick to Frances Abington.

" HAMPTON,

" *January* 28, 1775.

" The famous French writer Fontenelle takes notice that nothing is so difficult to a man of sensibility as writing to a lady, even with just grounds of complaint.

However, having promised, I must answer your last
very extraordinary note. You accuse me of incivility
for writing to you through Mr. Hopkins. Did not
Mrs. Abington begin that mode of correspondence ?
and without saying a word to me, did she not send
back her part in the new comedy, and say that she
had settled that matter with Mr. Cumberland ?
Could a greater affront be offered to any manager ?
And was not your proposing to Mr. Hopkins that you
would speak my epilogue written for the character,
while *another person* was to perform the part, not only
mere mockery of me, but destroying the play at
once. Let your warmest and most partial friend
decide between us. Whenever you are really ill, I
feel both for you and myself ; but the servant said
last Wednesday, that you *were well and had a great
deal of company.*

" You mention *your great fatigue.* What is the
stage come to, if I must continually hear of your *hard
labour*, when from the beginning of the season to
this time you have not played more than twice a
week !

" Mrs. Oldfield performed Lady Townley for twenty-
nine nights successively. Let us now examine how
just and genteel your complaint is against me. I
promised you I would procure a character of consequence to be written on purpose for you, and that it
should be your own fault if you were not on the
highest pinnacle of your profession. I have been
at great pains, and you know it, to be good as my
word.

" I directed and assisted the author to make a small character a very considerable one for you, I spared no expense in dresses, music, scenes, and decorations for the piece, and now the *fatigue of acting* this character is very unjustly, as well as unkindly brought against me.

" Had you played this part *forty* times instead of *twenty*, my gains would be less than by any other successful play I have produced in my management.

" The greatest favour I can confer upon an actress is to give her the best character in a favourite piece ; and the longer it runs, the more merit I have with her, and ought to receive her *thanks* instead of *complaints*. In short, Madam, *if you play*, you are uneasy, and if you *do not*, you are more so. After what you said to Mr. Becket, and what I promised, I little thought to have your *farce* drawn in to make up the bundle of complaints. However, to make an end of this disagreeable business, as the piece is written out, I am now ready to do it, and that you may have Palmer, I will give up the revived comedy ; but even this, I know, will not satisfy you—nor can you fix in your mind *what will*.

" Were I to look back what *real* complaints have I to make for leading me into a fool's paradise last summer about a certain comedy ! and an alarming secret you told me lately of a disagreeable quarrel. On my return home the same morning I met one of the parties, and instead of a quarrel between them, they were upon the best of terms, had never had the least difference, and Mr. M. [Murphy] was writing at Mr. T. [ighe]'s desire a prologue for his friend [Jephson's] new tragedy.

"Mr. Garrick most solemnly assures Mrs. Abington that nobody has in the least influenced him in this affair, and he hopes the above recital will convince her of the truth of his assertion."

Frances Abington to David Garrick.

"*Monday night, March* 6, 1775.

"Mr. Garrick behaves with so much unprovoked hostility to Mrs. Abington, that she is at a loss how to account for it, and her health and spirit are so much hurt by it, that she is not able to say *what* or when she can play. If he had been pleased to have given her a day's notice, she could have played her part in *The West Indian;* but it was not possible for her at three o'clock to read her part, get her clothes ready, and find a hair-dresser all by six o'clock, and that too at a time when she is in a very weak and ill state of health.

"If Mr. Garrick really thinks Mrs. Abington so bad a subject as he is pleased to describe her in all the companies he goes into, she thinks his remedy is very easy, and is willing on her part to release him from so great an inconvenience as soon as he pleases, and only begs, while he is pleased to continue her in his theatre, that he will not treat her with so much harshness as he has lately done."

David Garrick to Frances Abington.

" ADELPHI,

" *March 7, 1775.*

" MADAM,

" Whether [it be] a consciousness of your un-
accountable and unwarrantable behaviour to me, or
that you have really heard of my *description of you* in
all companies, I will not enquire ; whatever I have
said I will justify, for I always speak the truth. Is it
possible for me to describe you as your note of yesterday describes yourself ? You want a day's notice
to perform a character you played originally, and
which you have appeared in several times this season :
you knew our distress yesterday, almost as soon as I
did, and did not plead the want of a day's notice,
clothes, hair-dresser, etc., but you refused on account
of your health, though you were in spirits and rehears-
ing a new farce. You suffered us to be obliged to
another lady, of another house, to do your business,
when neither our distresses, the credit of the theatre,
or your own duty and justice, could have the least
influence upon you. How could I give you a day's
notice when I knew not of Mr. Reddish's illness but
in the morning ? and you were the first person I sent
to between *twelve and one,* and not at *three* o'clock.
It was happy for us that we found a lady, though not
of our company, who had feeling for our distress, and
relieved us from it without requiring a day's notice,
or wanting any thing but an opportunity to show her
politeness. These are serious truths, Madam, and are

not to be described like the lesser peccadillos of a fine lady. A little time will show that Mr. Garrick has done essential offices of kindness to Mrs. Abington, when his humanity only, and not his duty obliged him. As to your wishes of delivering me from the inconvenience of your engagement, that, I hope, will soon be another's concern : my greatest comfort is, that I shall soon be delivered from the capriciousness, inconsistency, injustice, and unkindness of those to whom I always intended the greatest good in my power.

"I am, Madam,

"Your most obedient servant,

"D. GARRICK.

"Your refusing to play this evening has obliged me, though but just recovered from a dreadful disorder, to risk a relapse."

Frances Abington to David Garrick.

"*Tuesday morning, March 7, 1775.*

"From your not recollecting some circumstances, your letter is a misrepresentation of facts from the beginning to the end.

"You are pleased to say *The West Indian* has been performed several times this season; it has really been acted but once, and that at the very beginning of the winter. You say I was well and in spirits at the rehearsal. Indeed, Sir, whoever told you so, deceived you; I was very ill, and not able to hold myself up in my chair. You say I knew the distress of the theatre at twelve o'clock. I saw very little distress, for it was plain that *The Country Girl* could have been acted from the instant that Mr. Reddish's illness was known; the design, therefore, of changing it to *The West Indian* could only be to hurt and hurry me; and if I refused, it was a good pretence for borrowing a performer to play my part, in order to give colour to the abuse that was intended for me in the papers this morning. I have, however, been too attentive to my business, and too faithful a servant both to you, Sir, and to the public, to suffer from such malice and ill-nature; and if you refuse me the indulgence that is due to me for all the labour and attention I have given to the theatre, for this winter in particular, and for many years past, I must at least remember what is due to myself; and if the newspapers are to be made the vehicles of your resentment, I must justify myself in the best manner I can."

David Garrick to Frances Abington.

" ADELPHI,

" *March 7, 1775.*

" I beg that you will indulge yourself in writing what you please and when you please. If you imagine that I in the least countenance, or am accessory to any scribbling in the papers, you are deceived. I detest all such methods of showing my resentment. I never heard of the disorder which was occasioned in *The Maid of the Oaks* : I was too ill to be troubled with it : and Mr. King, whom you have always

unjustly suspected, never mentioned it to me, nor
did I know of the paragraph you allude to till it was
shown to me this morning. Could *The Country Girl*
have been done with credit yesterday, I should not
have distressed myself to have applied to you, or to
have borrowed a lady from another theatre. As I
will always retract the most insignificant mistake I
may have made, I find by the prompter that *The
West Indian* has been performed but once. May I
venture, if *Braganza* cannot be performed on Thursday, to put your name in the bills for Lady Bab in
The Maid of the Oaks, or for any other part ? I most
sincerely assure you that I do not ask this to distress
you, but to carry on the business in the best manner
I am able."

" Mrs. Yates has not yet sent word that she cannot
play on Thursday, and I hope you may be excused.
I ask the question to prevent trouble to both.

" The writing peevish letters will do no business."

Frances Abington to David Garrick.

" *Thursday, two o'clock, 1775.*

" A paragraph to say that the *Sultan* is withdrawn
would be a very singular and a very new object :
however, as that threat is only meant in harshness
and insult to me, it is neither new nor singular, and
all the answer I should make to such a paragraph
would be that I had withdrawn myself from the
theatre, which I should most undoubtedly have done
some years since, but that Mr. Garrick has so much

real goodness in his nature that no ill effects need ever to be dreaded in a situation where he has the entire government.

" I will endeavour, and I think it is possible to be ready by Tuesday, as I see *The Sultan* is advertised for that day ; but I shall want many little helps, particularly in the business of the dinner scene, and about my song, as I am at best a bad stick in that line as well as in most others, God knows."

Frances Abington to David Garrick.

" *Wednesday morning,*

" *April or May,* 1775.

" Mrs. Abington has kept her room with a fever for some days past, or she would have complained to Mr. Garrick of a letter she has received from Mr. Hopkins, dictated in a spirit of incivility and misrepresentation. He says it is written by order of Mr. Garrick, which Mrs. Abington is the more surprised at, as she is not conscious that her conduct in the theatre has deserved so much acrimony and ill-humour. She apprehends that for some time past she has had enemies about Mr. Garrick ; and it is to them she supposes herself indebted for the very great change in Mr. Garrick's behaviour, after all the fatigue she has undergone, and the disappointments she has experienced in respect to the business that was by agreement to be done for her this winter.

" She hopes that Mr. Garrick has got some person to perform the part of Letitia in *The Choleric Man ;*

and in respect to the epilogue, she takes the liberty of referring him to Mr. Hopkins, with whom she left a message upon that subject.

Frances Abington to David Garrick.

" *Tuesday, three o'clock,*

" [April or May, 1775].

" Mrs. Abington presents her compliments to Mr. Garrick, and is very sorry to read of his indisposition ; she is very ill herself, and exceedingly hurt that he should accuse her of *want of zeal for the cause,* as she flatters herself that Mr. Garrick is fully persuaded she has never been wanting in duty and attachment to the business of his theatre.

" But she thinks she is entitled to the same degree of indulgence that is given to other performers, and hoped that Mr. Garrick would have had the goodness to let her come out in some stronger comic humour than that of Millamant [in *The Way of the World*].

" She begs that he will not be angry, or treat her with harshness, as he will certainly find her a very faithful and useful subject, if he will condescend to think her worth a very little degree of attention and consideration.

" She will play in *The Hypocrite* and *Bon Ton* on Saturday, if he pleases, and will be ready in *The Way of the World* the beginning of the next week ; but must trouble him for an answer if that measure is approved."

Mrs. Abington to Mr. Garrick.

"*Monday, May* 27, 1775.

" I am very much indisposed, and desire to be excused when I tell you I cannot act to-morrow night.

" If the consideration of the salary I receive is a reason for my being called out to play to empty benches, I must beg to decline receiving any more pay at your office ; at the same time I take the liberty of assuring you, that I shall be ready and willing to stay in town for the purpose of acting with you, if you think proper to call for my services, and in such case shall accept of any proportion of my salary that you may think I deserve for such attendance. I beg you will not take the trouble of writing an answer, as I am sure your spirits ought to be composed for the great business of this evening. I hope you are perfectly well, and am, with great respect,

"Your most humble servant,

"FRANCES ABINGTON."

Frances Abington to David Garrick.

"*Thursday, June* 29, 1775.

" I received the favour of your message by Mr. Hopkins, and have sent the farce as you was pleased to command.

" I am very certain that a few of your nice touches, with a little of your fine polish, will give it that stamp of merit as must secure it a reception with the public, equal to the warmest of my expectations."

David Garrick to Frances Abington.

" *July* 1, 1775.

" Mr. Garrick presents his best compliments to Mrs. Abington, and she may depend upon his doing his best to give her piece success. Had the author vouchsafed to have communicated with Mr. Garrick the matter would have been better managed."

Frances Abington to David Garrick.

" SOUTHAMPTON-STREET,

" *July* 14, 1775.

" I take this method of expressing my thanks for the very polite message you was pleased to send me by Mr. Hopkins, of which I beg leave to assure you I am entirely sensible.

" I am sorry to say I am as little read in *dramatic* as in other authors, but were I more conversant in this respect, I would not, in a theatre where Mr. Garrick is manager, take the liberty of catering for myself ; I can only say that the *parts* to which the actresses of *my time* have owed their fame are in the possession of other performers, particularly Beatrice, Mrs. Sullen, Clarinda, etc. ; and of those others in which I have been most favourably received by the public, the plays are so altered by the death of actors, the giving up their parts, or other accidents, that they are no longer of use to the catalogue.

" In the choice of new ones, therefore, I would certainly wish to be directed by you, nor will it be

wondered at that I am anxious for your assistance
in a point so very essential to my interest and reputation.

" Whilst you, Sir, continue upon the stage, it will
be the ambition of every performer to have their
names appear with yours ; I cannot therefore help
reminding you of your intention to play Don John,
and of your sometimes hinting that it was not impossible but you might appear in the character of the
Copper Captain.

" If such an event should at any time take place,
it would gratify my utmost wishes, in the meantime
I have only to hope that your present disposition in
my favour may continue, and I have nothing further
to desire in the world."

Endorsed : " Mrs. Abington about Pope's parts."

Frances Abington to David Garrick.

" SOUTHAMPTON-STREET,

" *November* 26, 1775.

" I am encouraged by the kind assurances you have
favoured me with, and from a conversation I was
accidentally engaged in last night with Mr. Murphy,
to be a little importunate with you on a subject which
has been the source of much discontent and unhappi-
ness to me.

" Mr. Murphy says his new comedy is not yet cast,
and flattered me much by assuring me it was your
opinion that it would be for the advantage of the
piece that I should be in it as well as Mrs. Barry ;

D

however, if the character which the author very kindly intended for me is to be given to that lady, from what I remember of it, I fear that I cannot undertake any other part without more disadvantage to myself than you would choose to lay me under.

" Permit me, dear Sir, to observe that if I had been at this time on a more respectable footing at the theatre, I apprehend Mr. Murphy would not have thought it necessary for the interest of his play to have withdrawn his promise to me in favour of any other actress ; and you will perhaps not think there is any very inexcusable vanity in this opinion when you are told that upon his showing me the complimentary verses on Mrs. Barry, which were afterwards prefixed to *The Grecian Daughter*, he was so obliging as to say that he would do as much for me if Mr. Garrick would let him—that is (as I understood it), if you received the play, the capital part of which he then designed for me.

" It is in your power, dear Sir, I know it is, at any moment to put me on such a respectable footing with the public, and, of course, with authors, that I should be thought not unequal to, nor be ill received in such light and easy characters of comedy as my talents confine me to : the part in question is one of these.

" I am not insensible to Mrs. Barry's extensive merit ; I know that she is singularly excellent in the pathetic : in the new comedy there is a character of that kind which might be made worth her acceptance. But I beg pardon, Sir ; I have perhaps said too much

FRANCES ABINGTON AS ROXALENA

After a portrait by Reynolds

on this point ; the end of my application is sufficiently obvious, and I flatter myself, Sir, you will not think it unreasonable or impertinent, but favour it with your kind attention."

David Garrick to Frances Abington.

" ADELPHI,

Friday, November 27, 1775.

" I am always happy to see the performers of merit, who belong to us, happy and satisfied ; but if I were to make myself uneasy when they are pleased, right or wrong, to be discontented, I cannot pay them the compliment to mortify myself for nothing. After I have said this, let me be permitted to say farther that I never yet saw *Mrs. Abington* theatrically happy for a week together ; there is such a continual working of a fancied interest, such a refinement of importance, and such imaginary good and evil, continually arising in the politician's mind, that the only best substantial security for public applause is neglected for these shadows. That I may hear no more of *this* or *that* part in Mr. Murphy's play, I now again tell you, that every author, since my management, distributed his parts as he thinks will be of most service to his interest, nor have I interfered, or will interfere, unless I perceive that they would propose something contrary to common sense. As I cannot think this to be the case between Mrs. Barry and you, I must beg leave to decline entering into the matter. I sincerely wish, for all our sakes, that you may have a character worthy of you, as well as Mrs. Barry. I can no more. You sometimes pay me the compliment to say that you would do anything I would advise; I flatter myself, if you had done so, you would not have repented of your politeness. I never advised you to play Ophelia, though that has been unjustly laid to my charge. I advised you to take Maria, and was polite enough to send you the play; you sent both the part and book back, with incivility to me, and great injustice to yourself. Mrs. Barry has discovered what you would not, and has taken it— wisely taken it. Remember to tell your friends that you *might* have played Maria, but *political refinement*, the bane of all our actions, prevented you. I shall in no wise hinder Mr. Murphy from paying you any compliments his friendship or kindness may intend you; and if they depended upon my accepting his play, I have done my part towards it, for it is accepted. I am sure Mr. Murphy means you well, and thinks justly of your talents; and I would not have you quarrel with him because his gratitude for the favours he has received in *The Grecian Daughter* may have made him willing to oblige Mrs. Barry by another part in his next play. Now, Madam, I have done. You wished to play *The Scornful Lady;* I fetched an alteration of that play from Hampton on purpose. I am very willing to do you all the justice in my power, and I could wish you would *represent me so* to persons *out* of the theatre, and, indeed, for your own sake, for I always hear the tittle-tattle again, and have it always in my power to prove that I am never influenced by any little considerations to be unjust to Mrs. Abington or any other performer."

Frances Abington to David Garrick:

" SOUTHAMPTON-STREET,

" *Friday night, November* 27, 1775.

" Your letter is very cross, and such a one as I had no apprehension I should provoke by what I intended as a respectful application for your favour and protection.

" Among the long train of accusations you unkindly urge against me, give me leave to exculpate myself of one only—I mean the charge of incivility to you in returning the part of Maria in *The Duel*. When you recommended that part to me, Mr. Hopkins gave me the play and desired I would return it in the morning ; it was then late at night. I gave it a hasty reading, and returned it accordingly, telling him I could not see much in the part ; however, I would play it if Mr. Garrick desired or insisted upon it. The part was never sent me : the charge, therefore, of my sending it back with incivility to you, must certainly have arisen from some misinformation.

" There is a coldness, a severity, in your letter, which at this time adds greatly to the affliction of your distressed humble servant,

" FRANCES ABINGTON."

Mrs. Abington to Mr. Garrick.

" [1775].

" Mrs. Abington has great complaints to make to Mr. Garrick respecting a servant in his theatre for very impertinently writing against her in the news-papers last night, only for begging to sit in the prompter's box to see one act of a play on a night that she was to perform in *Bon Ton*, when her head was dressed, ready to begin the farce, which was the reason she could not so conveniently go to any other part of the house."

Frances Abington to David Garrick.

" *Thursday, twelve o'clock,* [1775].

" The servant has brought me word that Mr. Garrick is very angry at my not attending rehearsal this morning.

" I do not believe him. I am sure, Mr. Garrick did not expect I could be able to go out this morning after the labour I have very willingly gone through for three nights past. I am ill to death, and really not able to stand; I cannot therefore think that much apology for my staying away is necessary, when the cause is so well known.

" I am not perfect in the part in *The Sultan*, and have been out of humour with it by being told that Mr. Andrews talks of the farce at the coffee-houses as the work of Mr. Kelly, which is so far from being a fact, that I declare to God Mr. Kelly has never so much as seen it ; and the report can only be meant to bring popular prejudice against it. I most sincerely wish that Mr. Andrews' farce was out, and had received that approbation which there can be no doubt of its meriting ; he would then perhaps not take the trouble of considering about who was the author of *The Sultan*, or at least not give to a gentleman who has never seen a line of it.

" I have once more to hope that Mr. Garrick will let it come out after Christmas, as the present powerful run of *Bon Ton* makes it very hard upon me, in the idea of being constantly upon the stage in two farces, one of which is like something dropped from the clouds, and only made its appearance at the benefits last year, or I should not have interested myself about the other, knowing the impossibility of my attempting that line of business while I am necessarily engaged in so many plays."

Frances Abington to David Garrick.

" *Sunday morning, ten o'clock* [1775].

" Mrs. Abington was surprised at receiving a message from Mr. Garrick last night respecting the part of Araminta, in *The School for Lovers*, as she had flattered herself that he understood her reasons for wishing to resign that character ; if he does not, she refers him to a note which she wrote to Mr. Bensley on Friday morning.

" Mrs. Abington takes leave to acquaint Mr. Garrick that she is very ill, and has been for some days, though she was not willing to trouble him with an account of her indisposition, nor would she wish to be excused from the business of the theatre when she is at all able to put on her clothes or walk upon the stage.

" She is greatly surprised to see *The Hypocrite* advertised for Wednesday, and begs it may not be continued with *her name* in it, as she certainly cannot play in it on Wednesday, indeed, if she was well enough to perform so long a part as that of Charlotte, Mr. Garrick knows that the play will not bring *half a house*, and it would be very hard that she should be obliged to play to empty benches merely to gratify Mr. Garrick's present resentment to her. Mrs. Abington told Mr. Garrick that she would play in any farce after *that* play that might be supposed to have strength enough to help to fill the house ; but his answer was, that *he was Manager.* She understands perfectly well his power as a manager, and is very willing to submit to it, when it is not exercised in endeavours to destroy her health, her peace of mind, and her credit with the public.

" She is willing to act in any plays that are ready, and can be creditably performed : if the plays are *not ready*, and that Mr. Garrick has no occasion for Mrs. Abington, she repeats the request she made last year, that he will give her up her agreement, and not make the *Morning Post* the vehicle of his resentment."

David Garrick to Frances Abington.

" *December* 5, 1775.

" I beg that you will keep Mr. Andrew's note, it is a justification to you ; and had he been guilty of the least endeavour to prejudice *The Sultan*, I would never have spoken to him again. Be assured I have done my utmost for the piece, and, had it not come out till Tuesday or Wednesday, we should, as well as you, have been great sufferers. I shall take care that you are kept from playing, till you appear in the new piece. We will settle the business of the table and guitar when we meet. I cannot attend you to-morrow, because I have a long and laborious part. On Saturday I shall attend, and settle the whole.

" I took care that Mrs. Wrighten should not have a gay song, nor do I understand it will in the least interfere with you—and don't be uneasy, a natural, gay, chansonette song, and natural ease and pleasantry, will be heard with pleasure, after the first embroidered air of a Farinelli : I believe an Emperor of the Turks was never seen before. Mr. Palmer will make his first appearance in *The Sultan*. If you would have Mr. Shaw oblige you most completely, a few half-guineas would be well bestowed, to have him home to your house and settle the song and accompaniments with you. Don't starve your business for trifles. I have done my utmost for the piece, and it will be most splendid in scenery and dresses.

" Yours very *truly*, when

" You are not *unruly*,

" D. GARRICK.

Frances Abington to William Hopkins.

" *Tuesday, three o'clock, January* 30, 1776.

" You will be pleased to let the manager know that I am ill (though I thank God I have not lost the use of my limbs, as he has been pleased to tell the public), but I am too ill to attempt to perform to-morrow night. My friends will take an opportunity of thanking Mr. Garrick for his humanity and civility, which you will have the goodness to tell him, and that I am his

" Most humble servant,

" FRANCES ABINGTON."

William Hopkins to Frances Abington.

" *Tuesday night, January* 30, 1776.

" I sent your letter to Mr. Garrick, who ordered me to inform you that he told no more than your servant delivered, and that he will both answer your letter and your friends at a proper time.

" As to the part of Lady Fanciful, both Mr. Garrick and myself have been informed that you said you never intended to perform it again."

" *Case.—Drury Lane.*

" LINCOLN'S INN,

" *March* 1, 1776.

" Mrs. Abington is engaged as a performer for the season at a salary and a benefit night. Benefits are generally fixed according to the rank of the performer, and that rank is determined by the rate of salary. The highest salary has the first choice of the day, and so on. Mrs. Abington stands in the fourth degree of eminence, Miss Younge the next.

" About a fortnight ago, when the benefits were fixing, Mrs. Abington had the choice of Saturday, the 16th of March, or Monday the 18th, for her benefit. She had objections to both : Saturday was Opera-night, Monday degraded her, for she then must give precedence to Miss Younge. After duly weighing these important points, rank and precedence prevailed over interest ; *she chose Saturday the 16th ;* and Monday was given to Miss Younge. The next day interest seemed to preponderate, and she rather wished for Monday ; but the night being engaged, and not to be had, she gave out that the managers refused to give her any night for a benefit, and she has hitherto declined to advertise, or make any preparations for, the 16th of March.

" The managers are somewhat distressed by this untoward conduct, though they are not concerned in point of interest, but should she not prepare for that night, there will be no performance.

" They have thought of giving her a notice to the following purport :—

" ' I am directed by the managers to acquaint you that, comformable to your choice of Saturday the 16th of March for your benefit, that day was allotted, and is kept for the purpose ; and you will consequently name your play, that it may be got ready, and other matters prepared in proper time. It may be right to inform you that, in consequence of your choice of that day, all others have been settled and fixed for the other subsequent performers, and that there is no other day vacant till Easter.'

" And if she persists in her stubbornness till a few days before the 16th of March, then to give her notice that a play will be performed in which she has a part, and which will be appropriated for her benefit. Or ought the managers to let the house be shut up and no play be performed ? Or, will this conduct of hers be deemed a waiver of her benefit at night ?

" *Counsel's Opinion.*

" ' I think the managers should send a person not interested in the house to inform her that the managers, observing she has made no preparations for her benefit, are desirous to know whether she intends to take that night or not, as they wish to prevent a disappointment to the town, by giving a play that night if she declines her benefit. This will produce an immediate answer ; whereas a notice may keep the managers in suspense. If she declines a benefit that night, the managers may give a play on their own account without any danger of being responsible to her for the profits. It may be thought candid on the part of the managers to make her an offer of any unappointed night, declaring they do it not from any obligation they conceive themselves under, but to convince her they have no design to take advantage of her refusal to accept of her benefit as a waiver of her right to one, which they apprehend it to be : if she refuses this offer, which is probable,

FRANCES ABINGTON
After a portrait by Reynolds

then I think she will have no colour to claim
a benefit.'

" JAS. WALLACE."

Frances Abington to David Garrick.

" LEICESTER-FIELDS,
" *March* 4, 1776.

" As it has been for some time my fixed determination to quit the stage at the conclusion of this present
season and not return to it again, I thankfully accept
your very obliging intention to play for my benefit
in May, you will therefore please to dispose of Saturday
the 16th inst. in any manner most agreeable to yourself.

" I am, Sir, your very much obliged and most
humble servant,

" FRANCES ABINGTON."

On this Garrick wrote : " The above is a copy of
the letter, examined word by word, of that worst of
bad women, Mrs. Abington, to ask my playing for
her benefit, and why ?—"

David Garrick to Frances Abington.

" *March* 7, 1776.

" At my return from the country, I found your
letter upon my table. I read it with great surprise,
and can yet scarce believe that you are in earnest.
It would, perhaps, be as vain as impertinent in me to
caution you against being too rash in determining
upon so serious a matter. My reasons for quitting

the stage are many, and too strong to be withstood ; you can have none but will be easily conquered by your inclinations. It will, therefore, be worth your while to consider seriously ; and if you have the least reason to repent of your last determination, the best night for a benefit, which is the last night of acting before the holidays, and which the proprietors have purchased, is at your service. If you are still absolutely resolved to quit the stage for ever, I will certainly in May do for Mrs. Abington what I have done for others who have made the same resolution."

Frances Abington to David Garrick.

" LEICESTER-FIELDS,

" *April 7, 1776.*

" Upon reading the paragraph which you were pleased to send me yesterday, two objections immediately started to me. I thought it might carry an air of arrogance, and be liable to expose me to censure, as making myself of too much importance with the public : and next, the style might be thought rather abrupt and impertinent. I wish for nothing more than to retire in peace, without any pretensions to that *éclat* which must necessarily attend *your* retreat.

" Mr. Lodge assures me that you were perfectly satisfied with the written declaration I sent you, and that you were so far from requiring any farther condition, as to declare you were ready to play for my benefit, even though my name should not be announced in the bills.

" Mr. Lodge waited on you a second time, to acquaint you, that I thankfully accepted your offer to play for me : and I confidently concluded, from the unfettered generosity of the above declaration, that this business would not be farther embarrassed by advertisements, or any other unnecessary conditions.

" I am, Sir, your most humble servant,

" FRANCES ABINGTON."

Garrick endorsed this : " A fal-lal from Mrs. Abington."

David Garrick to Mr. Lodge.

" HAMPTON,

" *Easter Monday,* 1776.

" If I am not mistaken, I have received a letter written by you, and signed by Mrs. Abington. Though this a little carries an air of ill-will to correspond with me by her solicitor, yet, as you are a gentleman, I shall rather think she does me a favour than an incivility. Upon my word, I cannot conceive what fetters I have put on my generosity by any advertisements I have sent her ; and if you will be pleased to unchain the lady (though she is apt to behave a little unruly to me), I shall be much obliged to you : indeed, Sir, without a figure, I most sincerely am at a loss to guess her meaning. If she does not choose to advertise as Mrs. Pritchard and Mrs. Clive did, pray let us have no more trouble about the matter, but let her please herself ; if she has any more to say, or to unsay, about this business, I shall be in town on

Wednesday morning, and a note from you shall settle it with me at least.

"'Varium et mutabile semper.'

"Be assured that I am quite satisfied with the declaration she has given me of her quitting the stage, and I am ready to fulfil my part of the agreement on the 7th of May; therefore I hope that it will be impossible for the most refined and active imagination to raise more doubts, though, if they should give me an opportunity of seeing you, I shall be a gainer, for I feel myself at this moment better for your recommendation of Dr. Miersbach."

Mrs. Abington had her benefit on May 7, 1776, choosing *The Stratagem*, in which Garrick played Arthur, and she, of course, Mrs. Sullen. She did, indeed, resign after this—but not for fourteen years; and even after, in 1797, she returned to the stage for two years. "A few weeks after her benefit it was announced, upon undoubted authority," so runs a contemporary account, "that she had taken an hotel in Paris, which was fitted up in a superior style, for the reception of the English nobility of both sexes, on their travels; and another week had scarcely passed before it was stated that she had given up going to France, and meant at the close of the year to retire into Wales for the remainder of her life." Actually, she played at Drury Lane during the next season, and remained at that house until 1782, when she transferred her services to Covent Garden for eight years.

Mrs. Abington now, more than ever, moved in social circles, and set up her carriage—probably the first English actress to do so. Also, she essayed to lead the fashion, as a contemporary has recorded :

" Mrs. Abington's dress boasted that elegant simplicity for which she has so long been considered as the priestess of fashion. She having long been considered in the *beau-monde* as a leading example in dress, her gown on Saturday night was of a white lutestring, made close to her shape, sleeves to the wrist, and a long train ; her hair was dressed very far back on the sides with curls below, and not high above, nor did she wear one of those tremendous hair frizzed peaks, which of late have disguised the ladies—so, probably, they will no more appear as unicorns with a horn issuing from their foreheads. Mrs. Abington is the harbinger of the reigning fashion for the season —a very beautiful style of petticoat of Persian origin is among the last importations of this admired actress. She, the pattern of fashion, has fallen into the absurdity of wearing red powder : her influence on the *ton* is too well known—let her at once deviate from this unnatural French custom, or, if she is determined to continue a *red head*, let her frizeur throw a little brickdust on the eyebrows."

In 1790 Mrs. Abington, as has been said, retired, without any parade, from the stage. She retired with a comfortable competence, which, it has been recorded, she much impaired by losses at cards, to which amusement she was prone. She was frequently entreated

E

to return to the stage, where she still had a large
following ; but she resented all overtures. The Margravine of Anspach, who is probably better known as
Lady Craven, amused herself with private theatricals
at Brandenburg House. When in 1796 the performance of *The Provoked Husband* was in preparation, the
Margravine cast herself as Lady Brute, and secured
the services of Mrs. Abington for Lady Fanciful. The
comedy was reduced to three acts, and while great
care was taken to preserve the importance of the
part of Lady Brute, that assigned to the actress was
whittled away to next to nothing. A rearrangement
of the play had hurriedly to be made, for Mrs. Abington
declined to play, unless the character of Lady Fanciful
was restored to its original value. In consequence of
this disagreement, Mrs. Abington's name does not
again appear in the Brandenburg House playbills
until May 31, 1797, when she again played Lady Brute.

She had returned to Covent Garden for the season
of 1797–98, and was warmly welcomed by those who
remembered her. Unless she was compelled by
financial troubles, this was unwise of her, especially
as she still insisted on playing youthful heroines.
Boaden had written of her in 1782 when she played
Lady Betty Modish : " In my opinion, nothing in
the art ever went beyond this performance. Her
acting bore the marks of great application and was
at once surprising and delightful. She seemed to com-
bine in her excellence the requisites for both the
fashionable lady and her maid. She was the most
brilliant satirist of her sex." When she reappeared,

however, he wrote : " Her person had become full,
and her elegance somewhat unfashionable ; but she
still gave to Shakespeare's Beatrice what no other
actress in my time has ever conceived ; and her old
admirers were still willing to fancy her as unimpaired
by Time as the character itself." It may be presumed
that the younger generation were not so content. She
played for the last time on April 12, 1799, taking the
part of Lady Racket in *Three Weeks after Marriage*,
the occasion being the benefit of Pope, with whom
she had acted for many years. She herself did not
take another farewell benefit.

Presently she was asked by a relative of some one
to whom she was indebted for a kindness to act for
her benefit.

" August 26, 1801.

" My dear Madam,

" The obligation I am proud to say I owe to
Mr. —— for the indulgent partiality with which he
has been pleased to distinguish [in his newspaper] my
exertion in my profession, calls upon me for every
acknowledgment that gratitude and sensibility can
inspire.

" It is, therefore, with infinite mortification that I
find myself under the necessity of refusing the request
made to me in your very polite and interesting letter ;
and I trust, my dear Madam, that I shall stand
excused in your opinion, when I assure you that if it
were given me to choose whether I would go upon the
stage, or beg charity from my friends, for my daily

bread, I would embrace the latter condition, and think myself a gainer in credit by the preference.

" In this state of mind, you cannot be surprised at my declining a visit to Brighton ; but I must not conclude my letter without saying that there is a passage in yours which I do not understand ; it seems to convey an idea that I have recently been, somehow or other, of use to your father. I would to God it had been in my power to show my gratitude, either now or at any preceding period of my life, to show my gratitude for his infinite goodness and friendship to me ; but hitherto this power has been denied to me, and it is only in poverty of words, as well as circumstances, that I have been able to acknowledge my many, many obligations.

" My spirits are very much hurt while I am writing upon this subject. You must, therefore, permit me to conclude with my acknowledgments to Mr. ——, and believe me, My dear Madam,

" Your very obedient and very humble servant,
" FRANCES ABINGTON."

Charles Dibdin, whose *History of the Stage* appeared in 1795, and who had, of course, seen her innumerable times, wrote of her as an actress with the utmost enthusiasm :

" With Mrs. Abington came a species of excellence which the stage seems never before to have boasted in the same perfection. The higher parts in comedy had been performed chastely and truly, perhaps in these particulars more so than by this actress. There was a particular goodness gleamed across the levity of Mrs. Pritchard, and by what one can learn of Mrs. Bracegirdle, who seems to have possessed the same captivating sort of manner which distinguished Mrs. Abington, she was in those characters natural and winning; but it remained for her successor to add a degree of grace, fashion, and accomplishment of sprightliness, which was no sooner seen than it was imitated in the politest circles. Mrs. Bracegirdle, let her merit have been what it might, did not perform Cibber's coquettes, and though that author waited for Mrs. Oldfield before he accomplished Lady Betty Modish, yet, however admirable she may have been in the representation of those characters, they did not appear to be so exactly in her way as Lady Townley and other parts which had a higher degree of consequence attached to them. Mrs. Abington kept critically to coquettes, and there can be no doubt, take the round of them through, and it is pretty extensive, that more uniform good acting never was manifested. . . . In addition to the grace, the ease, and elegance with which Mrs. Abington personated characters in high life, and aped politeness in chamber-maids, her taste in dress was novel and interesting. She was consulted by ladies of the first distinction, not from caprice, as we have frequently seen in other instances, but from a decided conviction of her judgment in blending what was beautiful with what was becoming. Indeed, dress took a *ton* from her fancy, and ladies both on the stage and off piqued themselves on decorating their persons with decency and decorum, and captivating beholders by a modest concealment of those charms which, in imitation of the French women, who never knew the sensation of a blush, the result of English feminine rectitude, our females now to the disgrace of the age, make it their study to expose."

Mrs. Abington long survived her retirement from the stage in 1799. At different times during her life she lived at No. 62 Pall Mall; in Southampton Street, off the Strand; in Leicester Fields; in Clarges Street, off Piccadilly; and in 1807 she occupied two rooms at No. 19 Eaton Square. Her husband died in 1806, and thereby her circumstances were improved, since the yearly allowance settled on him reverted to herself. John Taylor mentions that when he saw her in the last years she was wearing a common red cloak with the air and demeanour of the wife of an inferior tradesman. She died on March 4, 1815, being then in her seventy-eighth year.

SARAH SIDDONS
(*neé* KEMBLE)
1755–1831

SARAH SIDDONS (*née* KEMBLE)
1755–1831

I

BY both parents, Sarah belonged as of right to the stage. Her mother, who, born at Clonmell, in Ireland, on September 2, 1735, was Sarah Ward, daughter of that Ward who had acted under Betterton, and had afterwards become proprietor and manager of a theatrical company visiting the smaller provincial towns. In 1753 Sarah Ward married Roger Kemble, an actor fourteen years her senior : it has been said that Ward, who objected to his daughter marrying an actor, consoled himself by the thought that Kemble was none.

Sarah, who was born on July 5, 1755, was the oldest of the famous stage clan of the Kembles. "Her grandsire acted under Betterton and Booth ; her parents had played with Quin, she herself fulfilling a professional career which commenced with Garrick and ended with her performing Lady Randolph to Mr. Macready's Glenalvon." John Doran writes : " When I add to this record that she saw the brilliant but chequered course of Edmund Burke to nearly its close, and witnessed the début of Miss Fanny Kemble, the whole history of the stage since the Restoration seems resumed therein."

Sarah Kemble was born at Brecon, and an account of the house in which she was born has been handed down : " It is a public-house in the high street of this town, which still retains its appellation, ' The Shoulder of Mutton.' I perfectly well remember seeing it stand, with its gable front, projecting upper windows, and a rich, well-fed shoulder of mutton painted on the door, offering an irresistible temptation to the sharpened appetites of the Welsh farmers, who frequented the adjoining market-place, especially as within doors the same, or some similar, object in a more substantial shape, was always, at the accustomed hour, seen roasting at the kitchen fire, on a spit turned by a dog in a wheel, the invariable mode in all Breconian kitchens. In addition to which noontide entertainment for country guests, there was abundance of Welsh ale of the rarest quality ; and, as the ' Shoulder of Mutton ' was situated in the centre of Brecon, it was much resorted to by the neighbouring inhabitants of the borough. If I am rightly informed, old Kemble was neither an unwilling, nor an unwelcome, member of their jolly associations. Those who remember him tell me that he was a man of respectable family and of some small hereditary property in Herefordshire, and that having married the daughter of a provincial manager, he received a company of strolling players for her dowry and set up as a manager himself."

Sarah Kemble went on the stage as a child, though

SARAH SIDDONS AS THE TRAGIC MUSE

After a portrait by Reynolds

exactly at what age she first appeared is not known. There is extant a play-bill, dated February 12, 1767, in which Roger Kemble announces his company of comedians as playing at the King's Head, Worcester, with a concert of music. The play was *King Charles I*, written by the actor, William Havant. The characters were thus cast : James, Duke of Richmond, by William Siddons ; James, Duke of York, by Master John Kemble (then aged ten) ; The Young Princess, by Miss Kemble ; and Lady Fairfax, by Mrs. Kemble. In the following April, Sarah played Ariel, after which she appeared in many rôles.

When Sarah was about eighteen, in 1773, William Siddons, who was still with the Kemble company, fell in love with her, and she reciprocated the feeling. Mrs. Kemble would not sanction an engagement between her lovely daughter and a young actor with very indifferent prospects, the more so, because a neighbouring squire, one Evans, of Pennant, was anxious to make the girl his wife. Siddons, who was frantically jealous, proposed an immediate elopement, but Sarah, love-sick as she was, rejected the suggestion. Something had to be done. The young lover was dismissed, but was given a benefit at Brecon to help him on his way. On that night he interpolated a song called " The Discarded Lover," of which the first and last verses are :

> " Ye ladies of Brecon, whose hearts ever feel
> For wrongs like to this I'm about to reveal :
> Excuse the first product, nor pass unregarded
> The complaints of poor Colin, a lover *discarded*.

" Now your pardon he begs, as your pity he might,
But here till confess'd you have shown him to-night ;
For his merit, tho' small, you have amply rewarded,
To accept the poor thanks of a lover *discarded*."

The audience, who knew all about the affair, and
sympathised with the young people, heartily applauded
Siddons, and as he came off the stage the stately Mrs.
Kemble, in a towering rage, as heartily boxed his ears.
Before he went away Sarah promised to marry him as
soon as her parents' objections were overcome.

The girl, not to be behindhand, also left the company, and, according to the *Secret History of the Green-
room*, hired herself as lady's-maid to Mrs. Greatheed,
of Guy's Cliff, Warwickshire, at ten pounds *per annum*.
Her station there " was humble, but not servile," and
her principal employment was to read to the elder
Mrs. Greatheed. She always regarded herself as under
an obligation to this family, and would gladly have
repaid the kindness which the members of it had
shown her in her young days. Young Samuel Greatheed (who married Lady Mary, daughter of Peregrine
Bertie, second Earl of Ancaster) wrote a tragedy, *The
Regent*, in which he wished her to play the leading
part. She did not like either the play or the part. In
her distress she wrote to Dr. Whalley on September 1,
1787 : " Mrs. Piozzi may be an excellent judge of a
poem ; possibly but it is certain she has not of a
tragedy, if she really has an opinion of this. It certainly has some beautiful poetry ; but it strikes me
that the plot is very lame, and the characters very,
very ill-sustained in general, but more so the lady for

whom the author has me in his eye. This woman is one of those monsters (I think them) of perfection, who is an angel before her time, and is so entirely resigned to the will of Heaven that (to a very mortal like myself) she appears to be the most provoking piece of still life one has ever had the misfortune to meet. Her struggles and conflicts are so weakly expressed, that we conclude they do not cost her much pain, and she is so pious that we are satisfied she looks upon her afflictions as so many convoys to heaven, and wish her there, or anywhere else but in the tragedy. . . . Mr. Greatheed says it would give him too great trouble to alter it, so that he seems determined to endeavour to bring it on the stage, provided I will undertake this milksop lady. . . . Mr. Siddons says it will not do at all for the stage in its present state, for the poetry seems to be all its merit ; and if it is to be stripped of that—which it must be, for all the people in it forget their feelings to talk metaphor instead of passion—what is there to support it ? I wish for his own sake, poor young man, that he would publish it as it is." Bertie Greatheed's play was produced at Drury Lane on April 1, 1788, but though supported by Mrs. Siddons and John Kemble, it was, so says Genest, withdrawn after trying the patience of the public for nine nights. Mrs. Piozzi, who had a high opinion of it, furnished an epilogue.

Mrs. Siddons, it may here be remarked, had a keen sense of the stage. When, for her benefit on April 27, 1795, Samuel Rogers furnished her with an epilogue, she herself changed some of the lines.

Sarah Siddons to Samuel Rogers.

" MY DEAR MR. ROGERS,

"I know your goodness will pardon the liberties I have taken of curtailing and a little altering the ' Epilogue,' and though my having two long parts to perform upon my benefit night will make it painful to me to *speak* more of it, yet as you will probably let that appear among your other elegant productions, you will unquestionably *print* it as it was originally written. I am afraid my friends will think they have too much of a good thing, for I am desired by those whom I must not refuse to play Emmeline in *Edgar and Emmeline* (a fairy tale), and to speak the epilogue to it, so I think they will have *enough* of me, and all this (beside my part in the play which is quite new to me) I have got to learn. Pity and pardon, and believe me, my dear Sir,

"Your very much obliged

"And affectionate humble servant,

"S. SIDDONS.

"I send you the original ' Epilogue ' to compare with the copy, and as I think the trifling alterations I have, presuming on your kindness, made, will have a better stage effect, I hope they will not be disagreeable to you. Pray have the goodness to return it immediately, for, as Mr. S. Lysons would say : ' I must begin and study like a dragon.' "

A few months after Sarah had left home her parents, seeing that the case was hopeless, and sorely missing their eldest daughter, consented—though still with reluctance—to the marriage. This was celebrated on November 3, 1773, at Trinity Church, Coventry. On October 4 of the following year, their son Henry was born.

The young couple rejoined the family company ; but after a short while left to play, under the management of Chamberlain and Crump, at Cheltenham. There Mrs. Siddons's performances of Rosalind and Belvedera attracted much favourable comment ; and Lord Ailesbury was so much impressed that he recommended her to the attention of David Garrick. The story is continued by the actress in her *Autograph Recollections*, written by her in later days. It is clear, from the bitterness of the narrative, that she never forgave Garrick :—

" Mr. Thomas King, by order of Mr. Garrick, who had heard some account of me from the Ailesbury family, came to Cheltenham to see me in *The Fair Penitent*. I neither knew Mr. King, nor his purpose ; but I shortly after received an invitation from Mr. Garrick himself upon very low terms. Happy to be placed where I presumptuously augured that I should do all that I have since achieved, if I could but once gain the opportunity, I instantly paid my respects to the great man. I was at that time good-looking, and certainly, all things considered, an actress well worth my poor five pounds a week. His praises were most liberally conferred upon me ; but his attentions, great and unremitting as they were, ended in worse than nothing.

" How was all this admiration to be accounted for, consistently with his subsequent conduct ? Why, thus, I believe : He was retiring from the management of Drury Lane, and I suppose at that time wished to wash his hands of all its concerns and details. I, moreover, had served what I believe was his chief object in the exaltation of poor me—and that was the mortification of Mrs. Yates and Miss Younge, whose consequence and troublesome airs were, it must be confessed, enough to try his patience. As he had now almost withdrawn from it, the interests of the theatre grew, I suppose, rather indifferent to him. However that may have been, he always objected to my appearance in any very prominent character, telling me that the fore-named ladies would poison me, if I did. I, of course, thought him not only an oracle, but my friend ; and, in consequence of his advance, Portia in *The Merchant of Venice* was fixed upon for my début, a character in which it was not likely I should excite any great sensation—*I was, therefore, merely tolerated.*

" The fulsome adulation that courted Garrick in the theatre cannot be imagined, and whosoever was the luckless wight who should be honoured by his distinguished and envied smiles, of course became an object of spite and malevolence. Little did I imagine that I myself was now that wretched victim. He would sometimes hand me from my own seat in the Green-room, to place me next to his own. He also selected me to personate Venus, in the revival of *The Jubilee*. This gained me the appellation of Garrick's Venus ; and the ladies who so kindly bestowed it on me, rushed before me in the last scene, so that if Mr. Garrick had not brought us forward with him with his own hands, my little Cupid[1] and myself, whose appointed situations were in the very front of the stage, might have as well been in the island of Paphos at that moment.

" Mr. Garrick would also flatter me by sending me into one of the boxes, when he acted any of his great characters. In short, his attentions were enough to turn an older and a wiser head. He promised Mr. Siddons to procure me a good engagement with the new Managers, and desired him to give himself no trouble about the matter, but to put my cause entirely in his hands He let me down, however, after all these protestations, in the most humiliating manner, and, instead of doing me common justice with those gentlemen, rather deprecated my talents. This Mr. Sheridan afterwards told me, and said that, when Mrs. Abington heard of my impending dismissal, she told them they were all acting like fools.

" When the London season was over, I made an engagement at Birmingham, little doubting of my return to Drury Lane for the next winter ; but, whilst I was fulfilling my engagement at Birmingham, to my utter dismay and astonishment, I received an official letter from the Prompter of Drury Lane, acquainting me that

---

[1] This little Cupid was the subsequent autobiographer, Thomas Dibdin. He told Thomas Campbell, a biographer of Mrs. Siddons, as it was necessary for him to smile in the part of his godship, Mrs. Siddons kept him in humour by asking him what sort of sugar-plums he liked best, and promising him a large supply of them. After the performance, she kept her word.

my services would be no longer required. It was a stunning and cruel blow, overwhelming all my ambitious hopes, and involving peril, even to the subsistence of my helpless babes. It was very near destroying me. My blighted prospects, indeed, induced a state of mind that preyed upon my health, and for a year and a half I was supposed to be hastening to a decline. For the sake of my poor children, however, I roused myself to shake off this despondency, and my efforts were blessed with success, in spite of the degradation I had suffered in being banished from Drury Lane as a worthless candidate for fame and fortune."

Mrs. Siddons's eldest daughter, Sarah Maria, was born at Gloucester on November 5, 1775, and on the following December 29, at Drury Lane, Mrs. Siddons played Portia to King's Shylock. She appeared in that part, attired in a salmon-coloured sack and coat.

Presently, she was given the part of Euphrasia in *The Grecian Daughter*. Her Euphrasia, says Doran, "more nearly resembled an English than a Grecian matron in the costume. But she soon improved in taste, or was able to exercise her own without interference; and Sir Joshua approved of her innovation of appearing in her natural hair, without *marischal* powder—of a reddish brown tint, then in fashion, and worn with abundance of pomatum on the tubular curls of the ladies' head-dresses. She braided her locks into a small compass, in accordance with the shape and size of the head, and when long stiff stays and hoop petticoats were universally worn by stage heroines, as well as by ladies in general, Mrs. Siddons had the courage to appear in a dress far from ample, with a waist of the very shortest ; and King George III himself warned her against using white paint (*blanc d'Espagne*, I suppose) on her neck as dangerous to health.

It was not until February (1776) that Mrs. Siddons first appeared with Garrick, when he played his favourite character of Ranger in *The Suspicious Husband* to her Mrs. Strickland. Then he revived *Richard III*, and assigned to her Lady Anne. " She here met Roscius with all his terror," says Thomas Campbell. " Garrick's acting must have been startling. From what his contemporaries have said of it, we may guess that his impressiveness bordered upon excess. He made the galleries often laugh when he intended they should shudder. By his force, approaching to wildness, and the fire of his eyes, he dismayed the young actress. He had directed her, in speaking to him, always to turn her back to the audience in order that he might keep his own face towards them, and her forgetfulness of this direction was punished by Garrick with a glance of displeasure that unnerved her powers." This performance of *Richard III* was clearly a one-man show, for the *London Magazine* of May, 1776, after declaring that Garrick's performance beggared all description, added : " As to most of the other characters, particularly the female ones, they were wretchedly played. Mrs. Hopkins was an ungracious Queen, Mrs. Johnston a frightful Duchess, and Mrs. Siddons *a lamentable Lady Anne.*" This gives point to her story told in a letter from Horace Walpole (in 1782) to the Countess of Ossory, that when Mrs. Siddons was questioned about her transactions with Garrick, she said : " He did nothing but put me out. He told me to move my right hand, when it should have been my left. In short, I found I must not shade the tip of his nose."

It has been said that the reason that Sheridan did not invite Mrs. Siddons to return to Drury Lane was because he did not think her a first-class actress. Even the entirely unbiassed William Woodfall, of the *Morning Chronicle,* while thinking her sensible, held that she was not yet strong enough for London. Perhaps it was a blessing in disguise. Mrs. Siddons still wanted experience in leading parts, and this was more easily to be obtained than in the metropolis. In spite of her forebodings, she found no difficulty whatsoever in securing engagements in the provinces. In the winter of 1776 she was at Manchester, playing Euphrasia in *The Grecian Daughter,* Alicia in *Jane Shore,* Matilda in *Douglas,* Rosalind in *As You Like It,* and Lady Townly. Also she appeared as Hamlet, though that was a character she could never be prevailed upon to play in London.

From Easter to Whitsuntide, 1777, she was at York. " I never remember," says Tate Wilkinson, who acted with her, " any actress to have been so great a favourite at York as Mrs. Siddons. All lifted up their eyes with astonishment that such a voice, such a judgment, and such acting should have been neglected

by a London audience, and by the first actor in the
world. . . . In her Arpasia I recollect her fall and
figure after the dying scene was noticed as most
elegant ; nor do I recognise such a mode of disposing
of the body in so picturesque and striking a manner
as Mrs. Siddons does on such occasions."

John Henderson had strongly advised John
Palmer of the Bath theatre to secure Mrs. Siddons's
services, and he was wise enough to do so. So from
Manchester, she went to the Somersetshire watering-
place. " I now made an engagement at Bath," she
says in her *Recollections*. " There my talents were
encouraged by the greatest indulgence, and, I may say,
with some admiration. Tragedies, which had been
almost banished, again resumed their proper interest ;
but still I had the mortification of being obliged to
personate many subordinate characters in comedy, the
first being, by contract, in the possession of another
lady. To this I was obliged to submit, or to forfeit a
part of my salary, which was only three pounds a week.
Tragedies were becoming more and more fashionable.
This was favourable to my cast of powers; and, whilst
I laboured hard, I began to earn a distinct and flattering reputation. Hard labour indeed it was, for, after
the rehearsal at Bath, and on a Monday morning, I had
to go and act at Bristol on the evening of the same
day ; and reaching Bath again, after a drive of twelve
miles, I was obliged to represent some fatiguing part
there on the Tuesday evening. Meantime, I was
gaining private friends, as well as public favour, and
my industry and perseverance were indefatigable.

When I recollect all this labour of mind and body, I wonder that I had strength and courage to support it, interrupted as I was by the cares of a mother, and by the childish sports of my little ones, who were often most unwillingly hushed to silence for interrupting their mother's studies."—During her residence at Bath, Mrs. Siddons gave birth on July 1, 1779, to her second daughter, Maria—" I remained at Bath," she continues, " about three years, during which time Mr. Henderson came there to act for a few nights. He was most kindly encouraging to me, and, on his return to London, spoke of me most favourably. I acted Beatrice to his Benedict, and he commended my efforts even in comedy. He was a fine actor, with no great personal advantages indeed, but he was the soul of feeling and intelligence." Henderson said of her, even at this time, that " she was an actress who never had had an equal, nor would ever have a superior."

A few of the characters that Mrs. Siddons undertook must be mentioned, if only to show her versatility : Mrs. Candour, Rosamund in *Henry II*, the Queen in *The Spanish Friar*, Imoinda in *Oroonoko*, Lady Randolph in *Douglas*, Jane Shore, Lady Brute and Nell in *The Devil to Pay*. Her Shakesperean repertoire was already considerable : the Queen in *Hamlet*, Portia, the Queen in *Richard II*, Imogen, Isabella in *Measure for Measure*, Constance in *King John*, and, above all, Lady Macbeth, which she played for the first time at Bath in 1778.

II

Mrs. Siddons's success in the provinces had, of course, spread to London, and more than once shadowy offers had come to her from there ; but she was now making a fair and steady income, and, having three children for whom to provide, she did not see her way to give this up on the off-chance of glory. However, " in the summer of 1782," she says, " I received an invitation to revisit Drury Lane. After my former dismissal from thence, it may be imagined this was to me a triumphant moment. My good reception in London I cannot but partly attribute to the enthusiastic accounts of me which the amiable Duchess of Devonshire had brought thither and spread before my arrival. I had the honour of her acquaintance during her visit at Bath, and her unqualified approbation at my performances."

Though delighted to be called to London, Mrs. Siddons was sad at leaving her good friends at Bath, where she had been for three years, and at her farewell performance took leave of them in an address of her own composition :—

" Have I not raised some expectations here ?—
Wrote by herself ?—What, authoress and player ?—
True, we have heard her—thus I guess'd you'd say—
With decency recite another's lay ;
But never heard, nor ever could we dream,
Herself had sipp'd the Heliconian stream.
Perhaps you'd farther say—' Excuse me, pray,
For thus supposing all that you might say.
What will she treat of in this same address ?
Is it to show her learning ?—Can you guess ? '

Here let me answer—No, far different views
Possess'd my soul, and fired my virgin Muse ;
'Twas honest gratitude, at whose request
Shamed be the heart that will not do its best.
The time draws nigh when I must bid adieu
To this delightful spot—nay, ev'n to you—
To you, whose fost'ring kindness rear'd my name,
O'erlooked my faults, but magnified my fame.
How shall I bear the parting ?   Well I know
Anticipation here is daily woe.
Oh ! could kind Fortune, where I next am thrown,
Bestow but half the candour you have shown.
Envy, o'ercome, will hurl her pointless dart,
And critic gall be shed without its smart ;
The numerous doubts and fears I entertain,
Be idle all—as all possess'd is vain.—
But to my promise. If I thus am bless'd,
In friendship link'd, beyond my worth caress'd.—
Why don't I here, you'll say, content remain,
Nor seek uncertainties for certain gain ?
What can compensate you for the risks you run,
And what your reasons ?—Surely you have none.
To argue here would but your time abuse :
I keep my word—my reason I produce
                    [*Here her three children were discovered.*
These are the mites that bear me from your side
Where I was rooted—where I could have died.
Stand forth, you elves, and plead your mother's cause :
Ye little magnets, whose soft influence draws
Me from a point where every gentle breeze
Wafted my bark to happiness and ease—
Sends me adventures on a larger main,
In hopes that you may profit by my gain.
Have I been too hasty ?—am I then to blame ?—
Answer, all ye who own a parent's name.
Thus have I tired you with an untrained Muse,
Who for your favour still most humbly sues,
That you, for classic learning, will receive
My soul's best wishes, which I freely give—
For polished periods round, and touched with art,
The fervent offering of my grateful heart.' "

Let Mrs. Siddons, in her own words, tell the story of her reappearance in London :

" I was truly grieved to leave my kind friends at Bath, and was also fearful that the power of my voice was not equal to filling a London theatre. My friends, too, were also doubtful ; but I soon had reason to believe that the bad construction of the Bath theatre, and not the weakness of my voice, was the cause of our mutual fears. On October 10, 1782, I made my first new appearance at Drury Lane, with my own dear beautiful boy, Henry, then but eight years old, in Southerne's tragedy of *Isabella* [which was, in fact, Garrick's version of Thomas Southerne's *The Fatal Marriage*]. This character was judiciously recommended to me by my kind friend Mr. Sheridan, the father of Richard Brinsley Sheridan, who had seen me in that play at Bath. The interest he took in my success was like that of a father.

" For a whole fortnight before this (to me) memorable day—[her reappearance at Drury Lane]—I suffered from nervous agitation more than can be imagined. No wonder ! for my own fate, and that of my little family, hung upon it. I had quitted Bath, where all my efforts had been successful, and I feared lest a second failure in London might influence the public mind greatly to my prejudice, in the event of my return from Drury Lane, disgraced as I formerly had been.

" In due course I was summoned to the rehearsal of *Isabella.* Who can imagine my terror ? I feared to

utter a sound above an audible whisper; but by
degrees enthusiasm cheered me into a forgetfulness
of my fears, and I unconsciously threw out my voice,
which failed not to be heard in the remotest part of
the house, by a friend who kindly undertook to ascertain the happy circumstance. The countenances, no
less than tears and flattering encouragements of my
companions, emboldened me more and more, and the
second rehearsal was even more affecting than the
first. Mr. King, who was then manager, was loud in
his applause. This second rehearsal took place on
October 8, and on the evening of that day I was seized
with a nervous hoarseness which made me extremely
wretched; for I dreaded being obliged to defer my
appearance on the 10th, longing, as I most earnestly
did, at least to know the worst. I went to bed,
therefore, in a state of dreadful suspense. Awaking
the next morning, however, though out of restless,
unrefreshing sleep, I found, upon speaking to my
husband, that my voice was very much clearer. This,
of course, was a great comfort to me; and, moreover,
the sun, which had been completely obscured for many
days, shone brightly through my curtains. I hailed it,
though tearfully, yet thankfully, as a happy omen;
and even now I am not ashamed of this (as it may
perhaps be called) childish superstition.

"On the morning of October 10th my voice was,
very happily, perfectly restored, and again 'the blessed
sun shone brightly on me.' On this eventful day my
father arrived to comfort me, and to be a witness of
my trial. He accompanied me to my dressing-room

SARAH SIDDONS AS LADY MACBETH

at the theatre. There he left me; and I, on one of
what I call my desperate tranquillities, which usually
impress me under terrific circumstances, there completed my dress, to the astonishment of my attendants, without uttering one word, though often sighing
most profoundly.

" At length, I was called to my fiery trial. I found
my venerable father behind the scenes, little less
agitated than myself. The awful consciousness that
one is the sole object of attention to that immense
space, lined as it were with human intellect from top
to bottom, and all around, may perhaps be imagined,
but can never be described, and by me can never be
forgotten.

" Of the general effect of this night's performance
I need not speak, it has already been publicly recorded.
I reached my own quiet fireside, on retiring from the
scene of reiterated shouts and plaudits. I was half
dead, and my joy and thankfulness were of too solemn
and overpowering a nature to admit of words, or even
tears. My father, my husband, and myself sat down
to a frugal meat supper, in a silence uninterrupted,
except by exclamations of gladness from Mr. Siddons.
My father enjoyed his refreshments, but occasionally
stopped short, and, laying down his knife and fork,
lifting up his venerable face, and throwing back his
silver hair, gave way to tears of happiness. We soon
parted for the night; and I, worn out with continually
broken rest and laborious exertion, after an hour's
retrospection (who can conceive the intenseness of that
reverie ?), fell into a sweet and profound sleep which

lasted to the middle of the next day. I arose alert in mind and body."

That Mrs. Siddons had arrived, there was but one opinion. The public gave proof of it by filling the theatre every time *Isabella* was played—it was performed no less than eight times between the 10th and the 30th of August. The management of Drury Lane expressed its delight in a way most agreeable to the actress. " I was highly gratified," she says, " by a removal from my very indifferent and inconvenient dressing-room to one on the stage-floor, instead of climbing a long staircase; and this room (oh, unexpected happiness !) had been Garrick's dressing-room. It is impossible to conceive my gratification when I saw my own figure in the selfsame glass which had so often reflected the face and form of that unrivalled genius; not perhaps without some vague fanciful hope of a little degree of inspiration from it. . . . About this time I was honoured by the whole body of the Law with a present of a purse of one hundred guineas."

" Mrs. Siddons [as Isabella]," Horace Walpole wrote to the Countess of Ossory, " pleased me beyond my expectations, but not up to the admiration of the *ton;* particularly Mr. Boothby, who, as if to disclaim the stoic apathy of Mr. Meadows in *Cecilia,* was all bravissimo. Mr. Craufurd, too, asked me if I did not think her the best actress I ever saw ? I said, ' By no means ; we old folk were apt to be prejudiced in favour of our first impressions.' She is a good figure, handsome enough, though neither nose nor chin according to the Greek standard, beyond which both advance a good deal. Her hair is either red, or she has no objection to its being thought so, and has used red powder. Her voice is clear and good ; but I thought she did not vary its modulations enough, nor ever aproach enough to the familiar—but this may come when more habituated to the awe of the audience of the capital. Her action is proper, but with little variety ; when without motion, her arms are not genteel. Thus you see, madam, all my objections are very trifling ; but what I really wanted, but did not find, was originality, which announces genius, and without both which I am never intrinsically pleased. All Mrs. Siddons did, good sense or good instruction might give. I dare to say, were I one-and-twenty, I should have thought her marvellous ; but alas ! I remember Mrs. Porter and the Dumesnil—and remember every accent of the former in the very same part. Yet this is not entirely prejudice : don't I equally recollect the whole progress of Lord Chatham and Charles Townshend, and does it hinder my thinking Mr. Fox a prodigy ? Pray don't send him this paragraph too."

Walpole was, of course, nothing if not critical, and presently he wrote : " I cannot think Mrs. Siddons the greatest prodigy that ever appeared, nor go to see her act the same part every week, and cry my eyes out every time. Were I five-and-twenty, I suppose I should weep myself blind, for she is a fine actress, and fashion would make me think a brilliant what now seems to me only a very good rose-diamond." Yet, on December 30, 1783, he wrote to the Rev. William Mason : " I require a perfect tragedy at your hands, with no excesses in the construction, for all the rest I am in no pain; nor should be on that head had you not alarmed me. Mrs. Siddons, whom I have seen again, and like much better, though in that detestable play, *The Gamester*, shall do you justice, and Lord Harcourt will be in the third heaven between her and you."

Walpole did not actually meet her until January, 1788, when he wrote to the Countess of Ossory :—

" My histrionic acquaintance spreads. I supped at Lady Dorothy Hotham's with Mrs. Siddons, and have visited and been visited by her, and have seen and liked her much, yes, very much, in the passionate scenes in *Percy ;* but I do not admire her in cool declamation, and find her voice very hollow and defective. I asked her in what part she would most wish me to see her. She named Portia in *The Merchant of Venice*, but I begged to be excused. With all my enthusiasm for Shakespeare, it is one of his plays that I like the least. The story of the caskets is silly, and, except the character of Shylock, I see nothing beyond the attainment of a mortal ; Euripides, or Racine, or Voltaire might have written all the rest. Moreover, Mrs. Siddons's warmest devotees do not hold her above a demi-goddess in comedy. I have chosen Athenais [in Lee's tragedy, *Theodosium, or, The Force of Love*] in which she is to appear soon ; her scorn is admirable."

A greater expert than Walpole on the theatre in all its aspects, Thomas Davies, the biographer of David Garrick, describing her in his *Dramatic Miscellanies*, had nothing but praise of which to deliver himself. " The person of Mrs. Siddons is greatly in her favour ; just rising above the middle stature, she looks, walks, and moves like a woman of a superior rank. Her countenance is expressive, her eye so full of information, that the passion is told from her look before she speaks. Her voice, though not so harmonious as Mrs. Cibber's, is strong and pleasing ; nor is a word lost for want of due articulation. . . . She excels all persons in paying attention to the business of the scene ; her eye never wanders from the person she speaks to, or should look at when she is silent. Her modulation of grief, in her plaintive pronunciation of the interjection, ' Oh ! ' is sweetly moving and reaches to the heart. . . . Mrs. Siddons has in Belvidera, as well as many other parts, not only attracted the attention, but absolutely fired the favour, of the town in her behalf. This actress, like a resistless torrent, has borne down all before her. Her merit, which is certainly very extensive in tragic characters, seems to have swallowed up all remembrance of present and past performers ; but as I would not sacrifice the living to the dead, neither would I break down the statues of the honourable deceased to place their successors on their pedestals. The fervour of the public is laudable. I wish it may be lasting ; but I hope that

without ingratitude to their old servants, which will
make their passion for Mrs. Siddons less valuable, as
it will convey a warning to her, that a new face may
possibly erase the impression which she has so
anxiously studied to form, and so happily made."

James Boaden gives an account of Mrs. Siddons in
her prime : " There never was perhaps a better stage
figure than that of Mrs. Siddons. Her height is above
the middle size, but not at all inclined to the *embon-
point*. There is, notwithstanding, nothing sharp or
angular in the frame ; there is sufficient muscle to
bestow roundness upon the limbs, and her attitudes
are, therefore, distinguished equally by energy and
grace. The symmetry of her person is exact and captivating. Her face is peculiarly happy, the features
being finely formed, though strong, and never for an
instant seeming overcharged, like the Italian faces,
nor coarse and unfeminine under whatever impulse.
On the contrary, it is so thoroughly harmonised when
quiescent, and so expressive when impassioned, that
most people think her more beautiful than she is. So
great, too, is the flexibility of her countenance that
the rapid transitions of passion are given with a variety
and effect that never tire upon the eye. Her voice is
naturally plaintive, and a tender melancholy in her
level speaking denotes a being devoted to tragedy ;
yet this seemingly settled quality of voice becomes
at will sonorous or piercing, overwhelms with rage,
or in its wild shriek absolutely harrows up the soul.
Her sorrow, too, is never childish ; her lamentation
has a dignity which belongs, I think, to no other

woman; it claims your respect along with your tears.
Her eye is brilliant and varying like the diamond;
it is singularly well placed; 'it *pries*,' in Shakespeare's language, 'through the portal of the head,'
and has every aid from brows flexible beyond all
female parallel, contracting to disdain, or dilating
with the emotions of sympathy, or pity, or anguish.
Her memory is tenacious and exact; her articulation
clear and distinct; her pronunciation systematic and
refined. Nor has Nature been partially bountiful—
she has endowed her with a quickness of conception,
and a strength of understanding, equal to the proper
use of such extraordinary gifts. So entirely is she
mistress of herself, so collected, and so determined in
gestures, tone, and manner, that she seldom errs, like
other actors, because she doubts her powers or com-
prehension. She studies her author attentively, con-
ceives justly, and describes with a firm consciousness
of propriety. She is sparing in her action, because
English nature does not act much; but it is always
proper, picturesque, graceful, and dignified; it arises
immediately from the sentiments and feeling, and is
not seen to prepare itself before it begins. No studied
trick or start can be predicted; no forced tremulation
of the figure, where the vacancy of the eye declares
the absence of passion, can be seen; no laborious
strainings at false climax, in which the tired voice
reiterates one high note beyond which it cannot
reach, is ever heard; no artificial heaving of the
breasts, so disgusting when the affectation is percep-
tible; none of those arts by which the actress is seen,

G

and not the character, can be found in Mrs. Siddons. So natural are her graduations and transitions, so classical and correct her speech and deportment, and so intensely interesting her voice, form, and features, that there is no conveying an idea of the pleasure she communicates by words. She must be seen to be known. What is still more delightful, she is an original; she copies no one living or dead, but acts from nature and herself."

Mrs. Siddons's next part was Euphrasia in *The Grecian Goddess*, in which, had she not been over-ruled by the managers, she would have made her *rentrée*. During the season she played Isabella twenty-four times, Euphrasia eleven times; Jane Shore thirteen times, Calista, in Rowe's *The Fair Penitent*, fourteen times, Belvidera thirteen times, and Zara, in *The Mourning Bride*, twice. Her only failure—and that only comparative—was her Mrs. Montague in Thomas Hull's *The Fatal Interview*, which was only played three times.

Mrs. Siddons had become the rage of the town. When on December 14 she played Belvidera in *Venice Preserved* for her benefit, the receipts of the house were eight hundred pounds! The managers of the theatre were delighted by her success, which was so profitable to them, and they did their utmost to bind her to them. They raised her salary from five to twenty pounds. They also, as a further link, engaged her two sisters—Frances Kemble, who made her first appearance in London as Alicia on January 6, 1783, and Elizabeth Kemble, who, on March 1, played Portia.

Her second benefit, on March 18, when she appeared as Zara, was also profitable.

Also socially Mrs. Siddons was a great success. Her drawing-room in Gower Street was crowded, and " The First Gentleman of Europe " and other great personages, after the performances they attended, would go round to her dressing-room to congratulate her. Dr. Johnson was a fervent admirer. In October, 1783, she went to see him. " Mrs Siddons, in her visit to me, behaved with great modesty and propriety, and left nothing behind her to be censured or despised," he told Mrs. Thrale. " Neither praise nor money, the two powerful corrupters of mankind, seem to have depraved her. I shall be glad to see her again. Her brother Kemble calls on me, and pleases me very well. Mrs. Siddons and I talked of plays; and she told me her intention of exhibiting this winter the characters of Constance, Catherine, and Isabella, in Shakespeare." Kemble gave Boswell the following minute of what passed at this visit : " When Mrs. Siddons came into the room, there happened to be no chair for her, which he, observing, said, with a smile, ' Madam, you who so often occasion a want of seats to other people will the more easily excuse the want of one yourself.' Having placed himself by her, he, with great good humour, entered upon a consideration of the English drama, and, among other enquiries, particularly asked her which of Shakespeare's characters she was most pleased with. Upon her answering that she thought the character of Queen Catherine in *Henry VIII* the most natural : ' I think so, too, Madam ' (said he),

' and whenever you perform it, I will once more hobble
out to the theatre myself.' Mrs. Siddons promised
him she would do herself the honour of acting his
favourite part for him; but many circumstances
happened to prevent the representation of *Henry VIII*
during the doctor's lifetime."

Mrs. Siddons, happily, has put on record her meet-
ings with Johnson. " I do not exactly remember the
time that I was favoured with an invitation from Dr.
Johnson, but I think it was during the first year of
my celebrity," she says. " The doctor was then a
wretched invalid, and had requested my friend, Mr.
William Windham, to persuade me to favour him by
drinking tea with him, in Bolt Court. The doctor spoke
highly of Garrick's various powers of acting. When
Mr. Windham and myself were discussing some point
respecting Garrick, he said : ' Madam, do not trouble
yourself to convince Windham ; he is a very bull-
dog of argument, and will never lose his hold.' Dr.
Johnson's favourite character in Shakespeare was
Catherine in *Henry VIII*. He was most desirous of
seeing me in that play, but said : ' I am too deaf and
too blind to see or hear at a greater distance than the
stage-box, and have little taste for making myself a
public gaze in so distinguished a situation.' I assured
him that nothing would gratify me so much as to have
him for an auditor, and that I could procure for him
an easy-chair at the stage-door, where he could both
see and hear and be perfectly concealed. He appeared
greatly pleased with this arrangement, but, unhappily
for me, he did not live to fulfil our mutual wishes.

Some weeks before he died "—[Johnson died on December 13, 1784]—" I made him some morning visits. He was extremely, though formally, polite; always apologised for not being able to attend me to my carriage; conducted me to the head of the stairs, kissed my hand, and, bowing, said, ' Dear, Madam, I am your most humble servant'; and these were always repeated without the smallest variation."

George III, it is said, shed tears at Mrs. Siddons's acting, and the Queen commanded her to Court to read plays to their Majesties. If this was a compliment, it was also a trial, for the actress had to stand in the royal presence until she nearly fell to the ground with fatigue. " Peter Pindar," who never let miss an opportunity, mentioned this in his " Ode upon Ode; or, A Peep at St. James's " :

> " Ready to drop to earth, she must have sunk,
> But for a child that at the hardship shrunk—
> A little *prince*, who marked her situation,
> Thus, pitying, pour'd a tender exclamation :
> ' La ! Mrs. Siddons is quite faint indeed,
> How pale ! I'm sure she cannot read :
> She somewhat wants, her spirits to repair,
> And would, I'm sure, be happy in a *chair*.'
> What follow'd ? Why, the r-y-l pair arose,—
> Surly enough, one fairly might suppose,
> And to a room adjoining made retreat,
> To let her, for one moment, *steal* a seat."

The lack of hospitality shown to those who came to Court was combined with an equal penury in connection with those who were " commanded " to amuse the royal circle, and of some examples of this miserliness " Peter Pindar " is the historian :—

" For, not long since, I heard a forward dame
  Thus, in a tone of impudence, exclaim,
  Good God ! how kings and queens a song adore !
  With what delight they order an *encore*,
  When that same song, *encor'd*, for *nothing* flows !
  This Madam Mara to her sorrow knows !
  To Windsor oft, and eke to Kew,
  The r-y-l mandate Mara drew.
  No cheering drop the dame was asked to sip—
  No bread was offer'd to her quivering lip :
  Though faint, she was not suffer'd to sit down—
  Such was the goodness—grandeur—of the Crown !
  Now tell me—will it ever be believ'd ?—
  How much for song and chaise-hire she receiv'd ?
  How much, pray, think ye ? ' ' Fifty guineas ? ' ' No.'
  ' Most surely forty.' ' No, no.' ' Thirty.' ' Poh ! '
  Pray guess in reason—come again !—
  ' Alas ! you jeer us !—twenty at the least ;
  No man could ever be so great a b—st
  As not to give her twenty for her pain.'—
  ' To keep you, then, no longer in suspense,
  For Mara's chaise-hire and unrivall'd note,
  Out of their *wonderful* benevolence,
  Their bounteous M——s gave—not a groat ! ' "

The pecuniary treatment meted out to Madame Mara was also accorded to Mrs. Siddons, who was appointed preceptress in English reading to the Princesses—without salary—and came from the Palace, as Mrs. Delany puts it, " as rich as she went in."

" Such are the stories twain ! Why, grant the fact,
  Are *princes*, pray, like *common folk* to act ?
  Should Mara call it cruelty, and blame
    Such r-y-l conduct, I'd cry ' Fie upon her ! '
  To Mrs. Siddons freely say the same,
  Sufficient for such people is the honour."

It is only fair to say, that Mrs. Siddons not only made no complaint, but was very happy to go to Court. "To complete my triumph," she says, "I had the honour to receive the commands of their Majesties to go and read to them, which I frequently did, both at Buckingham House and Windsor. Their Majesties were the most gratifying of auditors, because the most unremittingly attentive. The King was a most judicious and tasteful critic, both in acting and dramatic composition. He told me he had endeavoured, vainly, to detect me in a false emphasis, and very humorously repeated many of Mr. Smith's, who was then a principal actor. He graciously recommended the propriety of my action, particularly my bold repose in certain situations. This, he said, is a quality in which Garrick failed : ' He never could stand still —he was a great fidgit ! ' . . .

" One could not appear in the presence of the Queen except in a dress, not elsewhere worn, called a saque or négligée, with a hoop, treble ruffles, and lappets, in which costume I felt not at all at my ease. When I arrived at Buckingham House, I was conducted into an ante-chamber, where I found some ladies of my acquaintance ; and, in a short time, the King entered from the drawing-room, in the amiable occupation of drawing the Princess Amelia, then scarce three years old, in a little cane chair. He graciously said something to one of the ladies, and left the lovely baby to run about the room. She happened to be much pleased with some flowers in my bosom, and, as I stooped down, that she might take them, if so disposed, I could not help exclaiming to a lady near me, ' What a beautiful child ! How I long to kiss her ! ' when she instantly held her little hand to my mouth to be kissed : so early had she learnt this lesson of royalty. Her Majesty was extremely gracious, and more than once during the reading desired me to take some refreshment in the next room. I declined the honour, however, though I had stood reading till I was ready to drop, rather than run the risk of falling down by walking backwards out of the room (a ceremony not to be dispensed with, the flooring, too, being rubbed bright). I afterwards learnt from one of the ladies who was present at the time, that her Majesty had expressed herself surprised to find me so collected in so new a position, and that I had conducted myself as if I had been used to a Court. Any rate, I have frequently personated queens.

" Afterwards I had the honour of attending their Majesties at Windsor also. The readings there were arranged in the apartments of my dear and honoured friend, Lady Harcourt, whom I had lately seen as the hostess of Nuneham, doing the honour of her splendid mansion, when the King and Queen and several of the younger branches of the royal family came, while I was on a visit there. They were so delighted with their loyal and noble host and hostess, and so charmed with all they saw, that their attendants were sent back to Windsor for what was necessary for three days, and even then they were loth to depart. One may imagine the usual style of magnificence in which they lived, from the circumstance that they were but little deranged by the unexpected arrival even of royal guests."

III

After four months, during which she acted at Liverpool, Dublin, and Cork, Mrs. Siddons returned to Drury Lane in October, 1783, and opened her second season, by Royal Command, with Isabella in *The Fatal Marriage.* Her detractors complained that she had not yet adventured in London in any of the characters of Shakespeare; and to silence these, she, on November 3, appeared as Isabella in *Measure for Measure.* Successful in this, she was soon seen as Constance to the King John of her brother, John Philip Kemble. How thoroughly she had studied the part may be gathered from her remarks on that character in her Memoranda :

" My idea of Constance is that of a lofty and proud spirit, associated with the most exquisite feelings of maternal tenderness, which is in truth the predominant feature of this interesting personage. The sentiments which she herself expresses in the dialogue between herself, the King of France, and the Duke of Austria, at the commencement of the second act of this tragedy, very strongly evince the amiable traits of a humane disposition, and of a grateful heart. . . . Again, in reply to the King's bloody determination of subjecting the city of Angiers to the sovereignty of her son, she says:

'Stay for an answer to your embassy,
    Lest, unadvis'd, you stain your swords with blood.
    My Lord Chantilly may from England bring

That right in peace, which here we urge in war ;
And then we shall regret each drop of blood
That hot rash haste so indiscreetly shed.'

" The idea one naturally adopts of her qualities and
appearance are, that she is noble in mind, and commanding in person and demeanour ; that her countenance was capable of all the varieties of grand and
tender expression, often agonised, though never dis-
torted by the vehemence of her agitations. Her
voice, too, must have been ' propertied like the tuned
spheres,' obedient to all the softest inflections of
maternal love, to all the pathos of the most exquisite
sensibility, to the sudden burst of heart-rending
sorrow, and to the terrifying imprecations of indignant majesty, when writhing under the miseries
inflicted on her by her dastardly oppressors and
treacherous allies. The actress, whose lot it is to
personate this great character, should be richly endowed by Nature for its various requirements : yet,
even when thus fortunately gifted, much, very much,
remains to be effected by herself; for in the performance of the part of Constance, great difficulties, both
mental and physical, present themselves. And perhaps
the greatest of the former class is that of imperiously
holding the mind reined-in to the immediate percep-
tion of those calamitous circumstances which take
place during the course of her sadly eventful history.
The necessity for this severe abstraction will sufficiently appear, when we remember that all these
calamitous events occur whilst she herself is absent
from the stage ; so that this power is indispensable

for this reason alone, were there no other to be assigned to it. Because, if the representative of Constance shall ever forget, even behind the scenes, those disastrous events which impel her to break forth into the overwhelming effusions of wounded friendship, disappointed ambition, and maternal tenderness, upon the first moment of her appearance in the third act, when stunned with terrible surprise, she exclaims :

> ' Gone to be married—go to swear a peace !
> False blood to false blood joined—gone to be friends ! '

—if, I say, the mind of the actress for one moment wanders from these distressing events she must inevitably fall short of that high and glorious colouring which is indispensable to the painting of this magnificent portrait."

It is impossible here to give the entire analysis of the character of Constance by Mrs. Siddons—the curious will find it in Thomas Campbell's biography of the actress—but enough has been printed to indicate the amount of thought she put into the representations of the characters she portrayed.

In the same season, Mrs. Siddons played, for her benefit, Lady Randolph in *Douglas*, thereby challenging, and successfully, Mrs. Crauford, who had been so successful in the part. For her second benefit, she chose James Thomson's *Tancred and Sigismunda*, in which the leading female rôle had frequently been undertaken by Mrs. Cibber.

Mrs. Siddons was overwhelmed with invitations to

this party and to that; but whenever it was possible she declined.

"I was, as I have confessed, an ambitious candidate for fame, and my professional avocations alone, independent of domestic arrangements, were, of course, incompatible with habitual observance of parties and concerts," she writes. "I, therefore, declined the honour of such invitations. As much of time as could now be stolen from imperative affairs was employed for various pictures. I had frequently the honour of dining with Sir Joshua Reynolds, in Leicester Square. At his house were assembled all the good, the wise, the talented, the rank and fashion of the age. About this time he produced his portrait of me in the character of the Tragic Muse. In justice to his genius, I cannot but remark his instantaneous decision of the attitude and expression of the picture. It was, in fact, decided within the twinkling of an eye. When I attended him for the first sitting, after more gratifying encomiums than I can now repeat, he took me by the hand, saying, 'Ascend your undisputed throne, and graciously bestow upon me some good idea of the Tragic Muse.' I walked up the steps, and instantly seated myself in the attitude in which the Tragic Muse now appears. This idea satisfied him so well, that, without one moment's hesitation, he determined not to alter it. When I attended him for the last sitting, he seemed to be afraid of touching the picture, and, after pausingly contemplating his work, he said, 'No, I will merely add a little more colour to the face.' I then begged him to pardon my presumption in hoping that he would not heighten that tone of complexion so deeply accordant with the chilly and concentrated musings of pale melancholy. He most graciously complied with my petition; and, some time after, when he invited me to go and see the picture finished, and in the frame, he did me the honour to thank me for persuading him to pause from heightening the colour, being now perfectly convinced that it would have impaired the effect: adding, that he had been inexpressibly gratified by observing many persons strongly affected in contemplating this favourite effort of his pencil. I was delighted when he assured me that he was certain that the colours would remain unfaded as long as the canvas would keep them together, which, unhappily, has not been the case with all his works. He gallantly added, with his own benevolent smile, 'And, to confirm my opinion, here is my name, for I have resolved to go down to posterity on the hem of your garment.' Accordingly, it appears upon the hem of the drapery."

"Sir Joshua," Mrs. Siddons continues, "often honoured me by his presence at the theatre. He approved very much of my costumes, and of my hair without powder, what at that time was used in great profusion, with a reddish brown tint, and a great deal of pomatum, which, well kneaded together, modelled the fair ladies' tresses into large curls like demi-cannon. My locks were generally braided into a small compass, so as to ascertain the size and shape of my head, which, to a painter's eye, was, of course, an agreeable departure from the mode. My short waist, too, was to him a pleasing contrast to the long stiff stays and hoop petticoats, which were then the fashion, and it obtained his unqualified approbation. He always sat in the orchestra; and in that place were to be seen, O glorious constellation! Burke, Gibbon, Sheridan, Windham; and, though last, not least, the illustrious Fox, of whom it was frequently said, that iron tears were drawn down Pluto's gloomy cheeks. And these great men would often visit my dressing-room, after the play, to make their bows, and honour me with their applause."

At the close of the season in the early summer of 1784, Mrs. Siddons visited Edinburgh, where she gave eleven performances. In recording this visit, she says: "How shall I express my gratitude for the honour and kindness of my northern friends?—for, should I attempt it, I should be thought the very queen of egotists. But never can I forget the private, no less than public, marks of their gratifying suffrages. There, I became acquainted with the venerable author of *Douglas*, with Dr. Blair, David Hume, Dr. Beattie, Mr. Mackenzie, etc., and passed with them a succession of fleeting days, which never failed to instruct and delight me. On the first night of my appearance, I must own I was a little surprised, and not a little mortified, at the profound silence which was a contrast to the bursts of applause I had been accustomed to hear in London. No; not a hand moved till the end of the scene: but then, indeed, I was most amply remunerated. Yet, while I admire the fine taste and judgment of this conduct on the part of an audience, I am free to confess that it renders the task of the actor almost too laborious ; because customary interruptions are not only gratifying and cheering, but they are really necessary, in order to give one breath and voice to carry through some violent exertions ; though, after all, it must be owned that silence is the most flattering applause an actor can receive." On one occasion, the silence was broken, after one of her great scenes, by a single voice exclaiming, " That's no bad," which ludicrous parsimony of praise convulsed the audience.

Mrs. Siddons has herself related her experiences in Ireland : " I took my leave of dear Edinburgh and proceeded to fulfil an engagement at Dublin. . . . This visit to Ireland answered all my expectations both of profit and pleasure. I was received by all the first families there with the most flattering hospitality ; and the days I passed with them will be ever remembered as among the most pleasurable of my life. The Duke of Rutland, however, the then Lord-Lieutenant, was very unpopular ; and upon one occasion, when I acted Lady Randolph, at his Command, the public displeasure against him was so excessively clamorous, that not one word of the play was heard from beginning to end : and I had the honour of participating in the abuse with the representative of Majesty.

" The manager of the theatre also very soon began to adopt every means of vexation for me that he could

possibly devise, merely because I chose to suggest, at
rehearsal, that his proper situation, as Faulconbridge,
in *King John*, was at the right hand of the King.
During the scene between Constance and Austria, he
thought it necessary that he should, though he did it
most ungraciously, adopt this arrangement ; but his
malevolence pursued me unremittingly from that
moment. . . . The theatre, meanwhile, was attended
to his heart's content, indeed, the whole of this engagement was as profitable as my most sanguine hopes
could have anticipated. . . .

" When my visit to Shane Castle was over, I entered
into another engagement in Dublin. Among the actors
in that theatre was Mr. West Digges, who had formerly
held a high rank in the drama, but who was now, by
age and infirmity, reduced to a subordinate and mor-
tifying situation."—[Rehearsing in July Pierre in *Venice
Preserved*, with Mrs. Siddons as Belvidera, he had a
stroke from which he never recovered, though he
survived two years. At this time, he was sixty-four.]—
" It occurred to me that I might be of some use to
him, if I could persuade the Manager to give him a
night, and the actors to perform for him, at the close
of my engagement ; but when I proposed my request
to the Manager, he told me it could not be, because the
whole company would be obliged to leave the Dublin
theatre, in order to open the theatre at Limerick ; but
that he would lend the house for my purpose, if I could
procure a sufficient number of actors to perform a play.
By indefatigable labour, and in spite of cruel annoy-
ances, Mr. Siddons and myself got together, from all

the little country theatres, as many as would enable us to attempt *Venice Preserved*. Oh ! to be sure, it was a scene of disgust and confusion. I acted Belvidera, without having ever even previously seen the face of one of the actors, for there was no time for even one rehearsal ; but the motive procured us indulgence. Poor Mr. Digges was most materially benefited by this most ludicrous performance ; and I put my disgust in my pocket, since money passed into his. Thus ended my Irish engagement ; but not so my persecution by the Manager, at whose instance the newspapers were filled with the most unjust and malignant reflections on me. At the time, I was on a visit of some length to the Dowager-Duchess of Leinster, unconscious of the gathering storm, whilst the public mind was imbibing poisonous prejudices against me. Alas ! for those who subsist by the stability of public favour."

Really in this instance Mrs. Siddons was unwarrantably used. She, who was so sensitive about her reputation as an actress, had played one of her great parts with a scratch company for the benefit of a sick comrade—and her reward was that a campaign of calumny was set on foot against her—she was avaricious, she was uncharitable, she was slow to lend her professional aid to unfortunate fellow-players, and so on.

William Siddons to the Printer [of various newspapers].

" *Thursday, September* 30, 1784.

" SIR,

" I am unused to write for public inspection, but I will not hesitate to state the truth ; and I think

H

the generous and candid will excuse the rest. I, therefore, declare that Mrs. Siddons never wished, asked,
or accepted a single farthing from Mr. Digges; and
that, a few days after his benefit, that gentleman
acknowledged his obligation to her by a very polite
note, which Mrs. Siddons (not expecting so malignant
an attack) destroyed.

" With regard to Mr. Brereton, so far from refusing
to perform for him, she agreed to do it for a much
smaller sum than she was to receive from any other
comedian, though every performer, for whom she
played, gave her considerably less than the manager
paid her nightly for twenty nights together; but just
as the benefits were commencing, she was taken ill,
and confined to her bed nearly a fortnight. When she
recovered, her strength would not permit her to perform immediately more than three nights a week;
and as the manager expected his engagement fulfilled,
and was to leave Dublin at a particular time, she was
obliged to forgo the performing for Mr. Brereton.
She, after that, made another attempt to serve him.
Why it failed, Mr. Brereton can truly tell; but I will
be bold to assert, without affording the smallest
ground for any charge against Mrs. Siddons.

" These are solemn facts, on which I leave the
public to judge. Animadversions on her public performance, and the questioning of her professional
talents, I shall ever submit to; feeling that those who
so liberally reward her exertions, have the best right
to judge of their degree of merit, and to praise, or
censure them, as they think proper; but all attacks

upon her private conduct that, if unnoticed, would undeservedly lower her in the estimation of the public, and render her less worthy of their favour and kindness, I hold myself bound to answer.

"WILLIAM SIDDONS."

This communication to the Press forced Brereton into the open, though his admission was made in the most grudging manner.

William Siddons to the Printer of the " Public Advertiser."

"SIR,

"By inserting the following (which will of itself prove my authority) in your paper of to-morrow, you will much oblige

"Yours, etc.,

"WILLIAM SIDDONS.

"'*William Brereton to William Siddons.*

"'SIR,

"'I am concerned to find Mrs. Siddons has suffered in the public opinion on my account. I have told you before, and I again repeat it, that to the friends I have seen I have taken pains to exculpate her from the least unkindness to me in Dublin. I acknowledge she *did* agree to perform for me at my benefit for a less sum than for any other performer, but her illness prevented it ; and that she *would* have played for me after *that*, had not the night been appointed after she had played three times in the same week, and *that* the week after her illness—and I am very willing that you should publish this letter, if you think it will be of the least service to Mrs. Siddons, to whom I owe many obligations of friendship.

"'I am, sir,

"'Your very humble servant,

"'W. BRERETON.'

"Mr. Siddons cannot withhold his public thanks from Mr. Brereton, for his obliging letter, and he has no doubt but that Mr. Digges will in a little time furnish Mrs. Siddons with another written testimony that will entirely confound the artful schemes of her detractors."

W. Brereton to the Printer of the "Public Advertiser."

"*October 5, 1784.*

"SIR,

"Having been informed that the letter signed by me in the several morning papers of yesterday, respecting Mrs. Siddons's conduct to me while in Ireland, has not been so clearly understood as it was both the intention on my part, and justice to her that it should, I think it necessary again to repeat, that it was in no respect owing to Mrs. Siddons, that I had no benefit in Ireland; but, on the contrary, that in the course of a long and dangerous illness I received proofs of friendship from her, which I shall ever recollect with gratitude, and avow now with sincere satisfaction.

"W. BRERETON."

West Digges now came forward with a letter saying, "that he had paid to Mrs. Siddons no money whatever, and had written a letter, expressing his obligation to her, and, as he understood this had been mislaid, he with great pleasure repeated his acknowledgments."

This sorry business was brought to a close on the evening of October 5, when Mrs. Siddons reappeared at Drury Lane.

"I had left London the object of universal approbation," she says, "but on my return, only a few weeks later, I was received, on my first night's appearance, with universal opprobrium, accused of hardness of heart, and total insensibility to everything and everybody except my own interest. Unhappily, contrary winds had for some days precluded the possibility of receiving from Dublin such letters as would have refuted those atrocious calumnies, and saved me from the horrors of this dreadful night, when I was received with hissing and hooting, and stood the object of public scorn. Amidst this afflicting clamour I made several efforts to be heard, when at length a gentleman stood forth in the middle of the pit, impelled by benevolent and gentlemanly feeling, who, as I advanced to make my last attempt at being heard, accosted me in these words : ' For Heaven's sake, Madam, do not degrade yourself by an apology, for there is nothing necessary to be said.' I shall always look back with gratitude to this gallant man's solitary advocacy of my cause : like ' Abdiel, faithful found ; among the faithless, faithful only he.' His admonition was followed by reiterated clamour, when my dear brother [John Kemble] appeared and carried me away

from this scene of insult. The instant I quitted it, I
fainted in his arms, and, on my recovery, I was thank-
ful that my persecutors had not the gratification of
beholding this weakness. After I was tolerably
restored to myself, I was induced by the persuasions
of my husband, my brother, and Mr. Sheridan, to
present myself again before that audience by whom I
had been so savagely treated, and before whom, but
in consideration of my children, I would never have
appeared again. The play was *The Gamester*, which
commences with a scene between Beverley and
Charlotte. Great and pleasant was my astonishment
to find myself, on the second rising of the curtain,
received with a silence so profound, that I was absolutely awestruck, and never have I been able to
account for this surprising contrast; for I really think
that the falling of a pin might have been heard upon
the stage."

On Mrs. Siddons's second entrance on that distressing night, she addressed the audience :

" Ladies and gentlemen, the kind and flattering
partiality which I have uniformly experienced in this
place, would make the present interruption distressing
to me indeed, were I in the slightest degree conscious
of having deserved your censure. I feel no such consciousness. The stories which have been circulated
against me are calumnies. When they shall be proved
to be true, my aspersers will be justified; but till then,
my respect for the public leads me to be confident
that I shall be protected from uninvited insult."

Mrs. Siddons never forgot, nor entirely forgave, that evening. " Here ended my disgrace and persecution," she says, with a not unnatural bitterness; " and from that time forth *the generous public*, during the remainder of the season, received my *entrée* each succeeding night with shouts, huzzas, and waving of handkerchiefs, which, however gratifying as testimonials of their changed opinion, were not sufficient to obliterate from my memory the tortures I had endured from their injustice, and *the consciousness of a humiliating vocation*."

William Windham to Sarah Siddons.

" OXFORD, *October* 10, 1784.

" I sincerely congratulate you on the victory obtained over malice and brutality the first night of your appearance. From Mr. [? French] Laurence, a friend of Sheridan's, who was present upon the occasion, and who is just come down here, I have received the whole account. Nothing has pleased me more than the style of your address, which completely removed any regret for the necessity of delivering it. It spoke the only language proper for the occasion— the language of innocence, disclaiming favour, and calling only for justice against calumny and outrage. I regret that I was not in the house at the time. You will now resolve, I hope, that the matter shall end, and that nothing shall provoke you to further explanation."

Sarah Siddons to William Windham.

"*January* 1, 1785.

" I wish you many happy returns of this day, and hope you will not be engaged this evening to tea, as I am to have a little music ; but my party does not exceed two gentlemen, who perhaps you know, with my own fireside. I am sure you would like it, and you can't be to learn that I am truly sensible of the honour of your society. I am flying to rehearsal, and shall flatter myself that you will give me the happiness of seeing you.

Windham was at this time on very friendly terms with Mrs. Siddons. Sir Gilbert Elliot, afterwards first Earl of Minto, writing to his wife on March 14, 1787, at a ball at Miss Adair's, mentions that the actress was the principal person there. " She did not dance," he remarks, " but was attended unremittingly by Windham, and Tom [afterwards Lord Chancellor] Erskine on the other side, and sometimes young Burke in front, and [William] Adams in rear." Windham's intimacy with Mrs. Siddons did not endure, however, for in his diary for May 27, 1805, after noting that he went to see her in *Zara*, he adds, " Had not seen her for years ; impression of her excellence not less than formerly."

Of all her admirers, the one that gave Mrs. Siddons most distress was that William Brereton, of whom mention has been made. He was married to Priscilla, daughter of that William Hopkins, prompter of Drury Lane theatre, who was so unmercifully plagued by

Mrs. Abington and, no doubt, many other actresses and actors. Those who loved not Mrs. Siddons hinted that, first, she had encouraged Brereton and then discarded him. It was to these reports that she referred in a letter dated March 13, 1785, written to Dr. Whalley : " I have been very unhappy ; now it is over, I will tell you so, that you may not lose the dues of rejoicing. Envy, malice, detraction, all the fiends of Hell have compassed me round about to destroy me ; ' but blessed be God who hath given me the victory,' etc. I have been charged with almost everything bad, except incontinence ; and it is attributed to me as thinking a woman may be guilty of every crime, provided she retain her chastity. God help them and forgive them ; they know but little of me." Brereton went mad, and tried to commit suicide at Dublin, owing, it was said, to his hopeless passion for Mrs. Siddons. He was placed in confinement, and died on February 17, 1787. His widow, on December 8 of that year, married Mrs. Siddons's brother, John Philip Kemble, and as Mrs. Kemble acted at Drury Lane and Covent Garden with her husband.

Years later a trouble, similar to that of the Digges-Brereton incident, arose—and, again, in Ireland ; but Mrs. Siddons was as little to blame in the one case as in the other.

Sarah Siddons to Frederick Edward Jones.

" Sir,　　　　　　　　" Dublin, *December* 8, 1802.

" I take the liberty of addressing you on a subject which has caused me much uneasiness. Public censure is, under any circumstances, well calculated to wound our feelings ; but it is particularly distressing when it is heightened by injustice.

" That reports, most injurious to me, have been circulated, can no longer be doubted, when I assure you that I understand it is generally believed I refused to play for the Lying-in Hospital. On this subject you will, I am sure, be as anxious to do me justice as I am solicitous to vindicate myself in the eyes of the public.

" I, therefore, beg leave to bring to your recollection, that you did me the honour of calling on me at my house in Park Street last summer, when it was liberally proposed on your part, as it was most cheerfully accepted on mine, that I should perform for some charity. You also recollect that it was considered by us both as a compliment justly due to Lady Hardwicke [the wife of the Lord-Lieutenant, Philip Yorke, Earl of Hardwicke], that she should have the *choice* of the particular charity, for which I was to perform ; and you thought it likely that her Excellency would give her preference to the Lying-in Hospital. You also, sir, must remember that I was not only willing, but desirous, of exerting myself for the benefit of so laudable an institution.

" Why so amiable a purpose was not immediately promoted, I cannot even guess ; but sure I am, that its postponement cannot be attributed to any backwardness on my part. The same motives which actuated me *then*, are no less powerful *now ;* and it will give me infinite pleasure, if, by the exertion of any powers I possess, I can be able to promote an important object of public utility.

"And now, sir, if I may be permitted to speak of myself as a private individual—I have only to regret the sad necessity imposed on me, of vindicating my character from the imputation of a failing as unamiable as, I trust, it is foreign to my nature. I regret that I should be constrained, from unfortunate circumstances, to endeavour to rescue myself from an obloquy, which I hope I have never incurred by my conduct.

"I regret that the country in which I am obliged to do so, should be Ireland.

"I have the honour to be, sir,

"Your obedient servant,

"S. SIDDONS."

IV

Within the compass of these chapters it is impossible to follow in detail the theatrical career of Mrs. Siddons, who was before the public for nearly half a century, and yet, on her retirement in 1812, was still the leading tragic actress on the British boards.

One, however, of her triumphs must be recorded— her greatest success, and the one with which she is still mostly associated—Lady Macbeth. An interesting analysis by herself of the character is printed in James Campbell's biography of the actress; but here our interest is more personal than critical. Mrs. Siddons had several times played the part in provincial theatres before she essayed it in London.

"It was my custom to study my characters at night, when all the domestic cares and business of the day were over," she says. "On the night preceding that in which I was to appear for the first time, I shut myself up, as usual, when all the family were retired, and commenced my study of Lady Macbeth. As the character is very short, I thought I should soon accomplish it. Being then only twenty years of age, I believed, as many others do believe, that little more was necessary than to get the words into my head; for the necessity of discrimination, and the development of character, at that time of my life, had scarcely entered into my imagination. But, to proceed, I went on with tolerable composure, in the silence of the night (a night I can never forget), till I came to the assassination scene, when the horrors of the scene rose to a degree that made it impossible for me to get further. I snatched up my candle, and hurried out of the room in a paroxysm of terror. My dress was of silk, and the rustling of it, as I ascended the stairs to go to bed, seemed to my panic-stricken fancy like the movement of a spectre pursuing me. At last, I reached my chamber, where I found my husband fast asleep. I clapt my candlestick down on the table, without the power of putting the candle out; and I threw myself on the bed, without daring even to take off my clothes. At peep of day, I rose to resume my task; but so little did I know of my part when I appeared in it at night, that my shame and confusion cured me of procrastinating my business for the remainder of my life."

Then came the time when Mrs. Siddons was to play the part at Drury Lane :—

" About six years afterwards, I was called upon to act the same character in London. By this time, I had perceived the difficulty of assuming a personage with whom no one feeling of common general nature was congenial or assistant. One's own heart could prompt one to express, with some degree of truth, the sentiments of a daughter, a wife, a lover, a sister, etc.; but to adopt this character, must be an effort of the judgment alone.

" Therefore, it was with the utmost diffidence, nay, terror, and with the additional fear of Mrs. Pritchard's reputation in it before my eyes. The dreaded first night at length arrived, when, just as I had finished my toilette, and was pondering with fearfulness my first appearance in the grand, fiendish part, comes Mr. Sheridan, knocking at my door, and insisting, in spite of all my entreaties not to be interrupted at this, to me, tremendous moment, to be admitted. He would not be denied admittance; for he protested he must speak to me on a circumstance which so deeply concerned my own interest, that it was of the most serious nature. Well, after much squabbling, I was compelled to admit him, that I might dismiss him the sooner, and compose myself before the play began. But what was my distress and astonishment, when I found that he wanted me, even at this moment of anxiety and terror, to adopt another mode of acting the sleeping scene. He told me he had heard, with the greatest surprise and concern, that I meant to act it without holding the candle in my hand; and, when I urged the impracticability of washing out that 'damned spot' with the vehemence that was certainly implied by both her own words and by those of her gentlewoman, he insisted, that if I did put the candle out of my hand, it would be thought a presumptuous innovation, as Mrs. Pritchard had always retained it in hers. My mind, however, was made up, and it was then too late to make me alter it; for I was too agitated to adopt another method. My deference for Mr. Sheridan's taste and judgment was, however, so great, that, had he proposed the alteration whilst it was still possible for me to change my own plan, I should have yielded to his suggestion; though, even then, it would have been against my own opinion, and my observation of the accuracy with which somnambulists perform all the acts of waking people. The scene, of course, was acted as I had myself conceived it; and the innovation, as Mr. Sheridan called it, was received with approbation. Mr. Sheridan himself came to me after the play, and most ingenuously congratulated me on my obstinacy. When he was gone out of the room, I began to undress; and, while standing up before my glass, and taking off my mantle, a diverting circumstance occurred, to chase away the feelings of this anxious night; for while I was repeating, and endeavouring to call to mind the appropriate tone and action to the following words, 'Here's the smell of blood still!' my dresser innocently exclaimed, 'Dear me, ma'am, how very hysterical you are to-night. I protest and vow, ma'am, it was not blood, but rose-pink and water; for I saw the property-man mix it with my own eyes.'"

On Christmas Day, 1782, Horace Walpole had written to the Countess of Ossory: "Mrs. Siddons continues to be the mode, and to be modest and sensible. She declines great dinners, and says her business and the cares of her family take up the whole of her time. When Lord Carlisle carried her the tribute-money from Brookes's, he said she was not *maniérée* enough. 'I suppose she was grateful,' said my niece, Lady Maria. Mrs. Siddons was desired to play Medea and Lady Macbeth. 'No,' she replied, 'she did not look upon them as female characters.'"

Clearly, during the next years Mrs. Siddons's mind had undergone a change, since she had selected Lady Macbeth for her benefit on February 2, 1785. During this season Mrs. Siddons played this character no less than thirteen times; and it may have been because of her success in it that her salary, which was ten guineas a week when she returned to Drury Lane in 1782, was now raised to twenty-four pounds ten shillings. Of course, there was criticism of the new Lady Macbeth.

Miss Seward saw the three great actresses; the first two in her younger days. She never forgot the clear, distinct, and modulated voice of Mrs. Pritchard, nor the pathetic powers, the delicate, expressive features, and the silvery voice, sometimes too highly pitched, of Mrs. Cibber. Mrs. Pritchard's figure, we are told, was then " coarse and large, nor could her features, plain even to hardness, exhibit the witchery of expression. She was a just and spirited actress; a more perfectly good speaker than her more elegant, more fascinating contemporary. Mrs. Siddons has all the pathos of Mrs. Cibber, with a thousand times more variety in its exertion, and she has the justness of Mrs. Pritchard, while only Garrick's countenance could vie with hers in those endless shades of meaning which almost make her charming voice superfluous, while the fine proportion and majesty of her form, and the beauty of her face, eclipse the remembrance of all her consummate predecessors."

Lord Harcourt missed in her Lady Macbeth " the unequalled compass and melody of Mrs. Pritchard ! In the famous sleep-walking scene his lordship still held Mrs. Siddons to be inferior—there was not the horror in the sigh, nor the sleepiness in the tone, nor the articulation in the voice, as in Mrs. Pritchard's, whose exclamation of ' Are you a man ? ' was as much superior in significance to that of Mrs. Siddons, as the ' Was he alive ? ' of Mrs. Crawfurd's (Barry's) Lady Randolph was, in the depth of anxious tenderness."

Whatever else could be said about her conception, it was at least a new reading. It won the approval of Lady Harcourt, who expressed her opinion at length :

" To say that Mrs. Siddons, in one word, is superior to Mrs. Pritchard in Macbeth, would be talking nonsense, because I don't think that it is possible ; but, on the other hand, I will not say with those impartial judges, Mr. Whitehead and Miss Farquhar, that she does not play near so well. But there are others, too, and in the parts for Mrs. Siddons, that are of this opinion : that she has much more expression of countenance, and can assume parts with a spirit, cannot be denied ; but that she wants the dignity, and, above all, the unequalled compass and melody of Mrs. Pritchard. I thought her wonderful and very fine in the rest of that scene. She throws a degree of proud and filial tenderness into this speech, ' Had he not resembled, etc.,' which is new and of great effect. Her 'Are you a man ? ' in the banquet-scene, I thought inferior to Mrs. Pritchard's ; and for the parts spoken at a great distance her voice wanted power. Her countenance, aided by a studious and judicious choice of head-dress, was a true picture of a mind diseased in the sleeping scene, and made one shudder ; and the effect, as a picture, was better in that than it had ever been with the taper—because it allows of variety in the actress of washing her hands ; but the sigh was not so horrid, nor was the voice so sleepy, nor yet quite so articulate, as Mrs. Pritchard's."

Doran agreed that, according to all accounts, Mrs. Siddons presented an original conception of the part. " She," he says, " imagined the heroine of this most tragic of tragedies to be a delicate blonde, who ruled by her intellect, and subdued by her beauty, but with whom no one feeling of common general nature was congenial ; a woman prompt for wickedness, but swiftly possessed by remorse ; one who is horror-

I

stricken for herself and for the precious husband, who, more robust and less sensitive, plunges deeper into crime and is less moved by any sense of compassion or sorrow."

Mrs. Siddons continued to act at Drury Lane for several years. It was rumoured that there were differences between her and her brother, John Kemble, who was stage-manager; but the fact of the matter was that it was next to impossible to get money from Richard Brinsley Sheridan, who was still " purse-manager " of the theatre. Instead, she toured the provinces, with excellent financial results. In the summer of 1790, she gave herself a holiday, and went with her husband to France, where they placed their daughters, Sarah and Maria, at a boarding-school at Calais. A second son, George, had been born on December 27, 1785.

" By solicitation and promise of punctual remuneration," Mrs. Siddons was induced to return to Drury Lane at the end of 1790, when she was received with a tumultuous welcome. When in the following March she played Jane Shore, " the languor of indisposition," says the *Morning Chronicle*, " was visible in her countenance; but this languor gave a deeper interest to the illusion, by making it more perfect, for it was suited to the distress of the penitent, and never did we see her sufferings more chastely, more calmly, and more impressively delineated." She was, indeed, so far from well, that she only acted seven times during the season, and created no new character. " Lady

ELIZABETH FARREN, COUNTESS OF DERBY

After a portrait by Sir Thomas Lawrence

Mount Edgcumbe and Mdlle. de la Villebazue have been here [Little Strawberry Hill] from Richmond this morning, and say Mrs. Siddons has suffered so much by her late exertions that she has relapsed, and they think must quit the stage," Mary Berry noted in her Journal, January 3, 1791 ; but it was not so bad as that, for she noted on April 3 : " Apropos to Catherine and Petruchio, I supped with their representatives, Kemble and Mrs. Siddons, t'other night at Miss Farren's," Mary Berry noted in her Journal for April 3, 1791. " The Hothams "[1] were there too, and Mrs. Anderson,[2] who treated the players with acting as many characters as ever they did, particularly Gunhilda and Lady Clackmannan.[3] Mrs. Siddons is leaner, but looks well. She has played Jane Shore and Desdemona, and is to play in *The Gamester :* all the parts she will act this year. Kemble, they say, shone in Othello."

It was about this time that John Taylor, the well-known journalist and the author of *Monsieur Tonson,* and an intimate friend of Mrs. Siddons, proposed that he should write her biography.

Sarah Siddons to John Taylor.

" NUNEHAM RECTORY, *August* 5, 1793.

" Indeed, my dear friend, if you were to write my praises with the pen of men and angels, I should shrink

---

[1] Sir Charles Hotham Thompson, married to Lady Dorothy Hobart, sister of John, second Earl of Buckinghamshire.

[2] Mrs. Anderson, daughter of Lady Cecilia Johnstone, married to a brother of Lord Yarborough.

[3] A nickname given by the writer to a lady of society.

from that celebrity which the partiality of so kind a biographer would confer : for how could I read without blushes those accounts of myself, which would be measures of his friendship, not standards of my worthiness. I am content that you should deceive yourself about my talents and my character, because I have an interest, and perhaps a livelier interest than most people, I believe, imagine, for the opinion of those who give themselves the trouble to think of me at all. But my friends in general are very much mistaken in my character. It has pleased God to place me in a situation of great publicity, but my natural disposition inclines me to privacy and retirement ; and, though the applause that is the palm of art, is necessarily sweet to my sense, yet sweeter is the still small voice of tender relatives and estimable friends. You may, therefore, tell me as much as you please of those talents with which you say I am so miraculously gifted, and I will hear you with pleasure, and pray for a continuance of your illusion. But do not, *I conjure you*, at least till opinion has a little more sanctioned the idea, do not bid all the world gaze, and wonder, and *certainly laugh*, at my yet feeble efforts.

"I am very much obliged to Mrs. [Mary Anne (" Perdita ")] Robinson for her polite attention in sending me her poems. Pray tell her so, with my compliments. I hope the poor charming woman has quite recovered from her fall. If she is half as amiable as her writings, I shall long for the *possibility* of being acquainted with her. I say, the possibility, because one's whole life is one continued sacrifice of inclinations, which, to indulge, however laudable or innocent, would draw down the malice and reproach of those prudent people who never do ill, ' but feed, and sleep, and do observances to the stale ritual of quaint ceremony.' The charming and beautiful Mrs. Robinson ! I pity her from the bottom of my soul !

" Pray go, and take Betsy to Marlborough Street, to see my bust of my little son, George. I could have done it better, but for the extreme heat of the weather, which made the clay crack and dry too fast. Adieu.

" Your affectionate friend,

" S. SIDDONS."

The next year (1794) was eventful, for on Easter Monday the rebuilt Drury Lane was opened. " Our new theatre is the most beautiful that imagination can paint," Mrs. Siddons wrote on April 11 to Lady Harcourt. " We open with *Macbeth* on Easter Monday. I am told that the banquet is a thing to go and see of itself. The scenery and dresses all new, and as superb and characteristic as it is possible to make them. You cannot conceive what I feel at the prospect of playing there. I dare say I shall be so nervous as scarcely to be able to make myself heard in the first scene."

Mrs. Siddons cannot have acted much during that season, for, on July 5, she was brought to bed of her youngest daughter, Cecilia. It may here be mentioned that Cecilia, who had a fortune of fifteen thousand pounds, married in 1833 George Combe, the phrenologist, who was six years older than she was. Combe was taking no risks. He examined the lady's head, and took the advice of Spurzheim as to his own fitness for the married state. Her " anterior lobe was large ; her Benevolence, Consciousness, Firmness, Self-esteem, and Love of Approbation amply developed ; whilst her Veneration and Wonder were equally moderate with his own." It is not surprising to learn that the marriage was thoroughly happy.

Sarah Siddons to a Friend.

"LONDON, *September* 11, 1794.

" My whole family are gone to Margate, whither I am going also ; and nothing would make it tolerable to me, but that my husband and daughters are delighted with the prospect before them. I wish they could go and enjoy themselves there, and leave me the comfort and pleasure of remaining in my own convenient house, and taking care of my baby. But I am every day more and more convinced, that half the world live for themselves, and the other half for the comfort of the former. At least, this I am sure of, that I have had no will of my own since I remember ; and, indeed, to be just, I fancy I should have little delight in so selfish an existence."

Mrs. Siddons, though not in want of money, was none the less angry that Sheridan did not meet his obligations to her.

Sarah Siddons to a Friend.

" *May*, 1796.

" Here am I, sitting close in a little dark room in a wretched inn in a little poking village, called Newport Pagnell. I am on my way to Manchester, where I am to act for a fortnight; from whence I am to be whirled to Liverpool, there to do the same. From thence, I skim away to York and Leeds ; and then, when Drury Lane opens—who can tell ? for it depends on Mr. Sheridan, who is uncertainty personified. *I have got no money from him yet ;* and all my last benefit, a great one, was swept into his treasury ; nor have I seen a shilling of it. Mr. Siddons has made an appointment to see him to-day at Hammersley's. As I came away very early, I don't know the result of the conference ; but unless things are settled to Mr. Siddons's satisfactioɩ, he is determined to put the affair into his lawyer's hands."

However, Mrs. Siddons did return to Drury Lane for the season 1796-7, but the financial conditions were no better. " I am, as you see, acting again ; but how much difficulty to get my money ! " she wrote to a friend on November 9. " Sheridan is certainly the greatest phenomenon that Nature has produced for centuries. Our theatre is going on, to the astonishment of everybody. Very few of the actors are paid, and all are vowing to withdraw themselves : yet still we go on. Sheridan is certainly omnipotent."

The next season (1797–8) found Mrs. Siddons still at Drury Lane, during which she played more than

forty times. She appeared in two new characters .
Julia in *The Rivals* and Mrs. Haller in *The Stranger*,
which last play, an adaptation from the German of
Kotzebue, was performed sixteen times within a
period of four months.

Sarah Siddons to a Friend.

"LONDON, *January* 7, 1798.

" I can get no money from the theatre. My precious
two thousand pounds are swallowed up in that drown-
ing gulph "—[Mrs. Siddons means Sheridan]—"from
whom no plea of right or justice can save its victims."

Sarah Siddons to Tate Wilkinson.

"LONDON, *May* 29, 1798.

" MY DEAR MR. WILKINSON,

        " My plans for this summer are so arranged,
that I have no chance of the pleasure of seeing you.
The illness of my second daughter, Maria, has deranged all schemes of pleasure as well as profit. I
thank God she is better ; but the nature of her constitution is such, that it will be long ere we can reasonably banish the fear of an approaching consumption.
It is dreadful to see an innocent, lovely young creature
daily sinking under the languor of illness, which may
terminate in death at last, in spite of the most vigilant
tenderness. A parent's misery, under this distress,
you can more easily imagine than I can describe ;
but if you are the man I take you for, you will not
refuse me a favour. It would *indeed* be a great com-

fort to us all, if you would allow our dear Patsy "—
[Wilkinson's daughter]—" to come to us on our return
to town in the autumn, to stay with us a few months.
I am sure it would do my dear Maria so much good;
for the physician tells me she will require the same
confinement and the same care the next winter. And,
let it not offend the pride of my good friend, when I
beg it to be understood, that I wish to defray the
expense of her journey. Do, dear soul! grant my
request. Give my kind compliments to your family,
my love to my own dear Patsy, and accept yourself the
best and most cordial wishes of

"S. SIDDONS."

Sarah Siddons to a Friend.
"LONDON, *June*, 1798.

"We are all going to Clifton, not because it is
thought good for Maria, but because she fancies that
place; and I know so well, from sad experience, how
powerfully the imagination operates on a feeble frame,
that I hope, from the indulgence of her little whim, to
reap some benefit from the journey."

Not all her mother's tenderness and care could
save Maria Siddons, who died in October, 1798, at
the age of nineteen, and was buried at Bristol.

Sarah Siddons to Mrs. FitzHugh.
"*October*, 1798.

"Although my mind is not sufficiently tran-
quillised to talk much, yet the conviction of your

undeviating affection impels me to quiet your anxiety
so far as to tell you that I am tolerably well. This
sad event I have been long prepared for, and bow
with humble resignation to the decree of that merciful
God who has taken to Himself the dear angel I must
ever tenderly lament. I dare not trust myself further.
Oh that you were here, that I might talk to you of
her death-bed—in dignity of mind and pious resignation, far surpassing the imagination of Rousseau and
Richardson in their Eloise and Clarissa Harlowe; for
hers was, I believe, from the immediate inspiration of
the Divinity."

Apart from the death of the second daughter, Mrs.
Siddons had other troubles about this time. She was
worried about money, for Sheridan had not yet
settled with her. Again, though for a good many
years her marriage had been happy, yet as time passed
her husband began to chafe at having to play second
string to his celebrated wife. The more famous she
became, the more he was relegated to the background—
not by her, perhaps, but by her friends and acquaint-
ances. He was so overshadowed by her at Drury
Lane, that, at last—and, perhaps, not unnaturally—
he retired from that theatre. He purchased an interest
in Sadler's Wells Theatre, but that proved an unfortunate investment, and his wife had to dip her hand
deeply into a depleted pocket. He was often at the
house in Marlborough Street, and there was not any
serious discordance between husband and wife.

Sarah Siddons to William Siddons.

"*December* 16, 1807.

"MY DEAR SID,

"I am really sorry that my little flash of merriment should have been taken so seriously, for I am sure, however we may differ in trifles, *we can never cease to love one another.* You wish me to say what I expect to have done—I can expect nothing more than you yourself have designed me in your will. Be (as you ought to be) master of all while God permits; but, in case of your death, only let me be put out of the power of any person living. This is all that I desire; and I think that you cannot but be convinced that it is reasonable and proper.

"Your ever affectionate and faithful

"S. S."

Siddons came to see his wife at her new home, Westbourne Farm, and she visited him from time to time at Bath. where he settled, and remained until his death on March 11, 1808, when she was playing at Edinburgh. She paid his memory the compliment of withdrawing from the stage for a fortnight.

Sarah Siddons to Mrs. Piozzi.

"*March* 29, 1808.

"How unwearied is your goodness to me, my good friend. There is something so awful in this sudden dissolution of so long a connection, that I shall feel it longer than I shall speak of it. May I die the death of my honest, worthy husband, and may those to whom I am dear remember me when I am gone, as I remember him, forgetting and forgiving all my errors, and recollecting only my quietness of spirit and single-ness of heart. Remember me to your dear Mr. Piozzi. My head is still so dull with this stunning surprise, that I cannot see what I write. Adieu, dear soul; do not cease to love your friend."

V

Mrs. Siddons often talked of retiring, but she was deterred by the fact that her brother John, who had been stage-manager of Drury Lane, had purchased a sixth share in Covent Garden, paying down £10,000 in part of the £23,000, its estimated value, leaving his profits to accumulate in Harris's hands to liquidate the balance. She thought it her duty, knowing her drawing capacity, to stand by him as leading lady. " Alas! my dear friend, what have I *here?* " she wrote to a friend at this time. " Yet here, even here, I could be content to linger still in peace and calmness. Content is all I wish. But I must again enter into the bustle of the world. For, though fame and fortune have given me all I wish, yet, while my presence and my exertions here may be useful to others, I do not think myself at liberty to give myself up to my own selfish gratifications." She repeated more or less this sentiment in August, 1803 : " I shall leave this place " —[Banisters, the seat of Mrs. FitzHugh's husband, near Southampton]—" on the fourth of next month, and will write again, as soon as I can, after I get to town. I shall have a great deal of business on my hands, and upon my head and heart many imperious claims. I find it is utter folly in me to think that I am never to live one day for *myself*, while these various claims, dear and tender as they must always be, exist : nothing but my *brother* could have induced me to appear again in public, but *his* interest and honour must always be most dear to *me*."

Her means not allowing her to retire, at the close of the season she again visited the provinces. The erysipelas, which was ultimately fatal in her old age, now began to attack her with a burning heat in her lips which was often very tormenting.

Sarah Siddons to Mrs. FitzHugh.

" Preston, *July* 14, 1801

" In about a fortnight, I expect to commence my journey to Bath. Mr. Siddons is there, for he finds no relief from his rheumatism elsewhere. His accounts of himself are less favourable than those of any one who writes to me about him ; but I hope and trust that I shall find him better than he himself thinks ; for I know by sad experience, with what difficulty a mind, weakened by long and uninterrupted suffering, admits hope, much less assurance.

" I shall be here till Saturday ; and after that time, at Lancaster, till Thursday the 28th ; thence I shall go immediately to Bath, where I shall have about a month's quiet ; and then begin to play at Bristol for a few nights. ' Such resting finds the soul of unblest feet.' *When* we shall come to London is uncertain, for nothing is settled by Mr. Sheridan, and I think it not impossible that *my* winter may be spent in Dublin; for I must go on *making*, to secure the few comforts that I have been able to attain for myself and my family. It is providential for us all, that I can do so much. But I hope it is not wrong to say, that I am tired, and should be glad to be at rest indeed. I hope yet to see the day when I can be quiet. My mouth is not yet well, though somewhat less exquisitely painful. I have become a frightful object with it, and, I believe, this complaint has robbed me of those poor remains of beauty once admired, at least, which, in your partial eyes, I once possessed."

Drury Lane, however, saw her again in the autumn of 1802.

Sarah Siddons to Mrs. FitzHugh.

" LONDON, *April*, 1802.

" Except for a day or two, the weather has been very favourable to me hitherto. I trust it may continue so, for *A Winter's Tale* promises to be very attractive; and, whilst it continues so, I am bound in honour and conscience to put my shoulder to the wheel, for it has been attended with great expense to the Managers, and, if I can keep warm, I trust I shall continue tolerably well.

" As to my plans, they are, as usual, all uncertain; and I am precisely in the situation of poor Lady

Percy, to whom Hotspur comically says, ' I trust thou will not utter what thou dost not know.'

" This must continue to be the case, in a great measure, whilst I continue to be the servant of the public, for whom (and let it not be thought vain) I can never sufficiently exert myself. I really think they receive me every night with greater and greater testimonies of approbation. I know it will give you pleasure to hear this, my dear friend, and you will not suspect me of deceiving myself in this particular.

" The other night had very nearly terminated all my exertions; for, whilst I was standing for the statue in *A Winter's Tale*, my drapery flew over the lamps that were placed behind the pedestal. It caught fire, and had it not been for one of the scene-men, who most humanely crept on his knees and extinguished it, without knowing anything of the matter, I might have been burnt to death, or, at all events, I should have been frightened out of my senses. Surrounded as I was with muslin, the flame would have run like wildfire. The bottom of the train was entirely burned. But for the man's promptitude, it would seem as if my fate would have been inevitable. I have well rewarded the good man, and I regard my deliverance as a most gracious interposition of Providence. There is a special Providence in the fall of a sparrow. Here I am, safe and well. God be praised! and may His goodness make me profit, as I ought, by the time that is vouchsafed me.

" My son Harry's success "—[his first appearance on the stage at Covent Garden]—" has been a great comfort to me. I do think, if I can divest myself of partiality, that it is a very respectable first attempt."

Sarah Siddons to Mrs. FitzHugh.

"LONDON, [later in] *April*, 1802.

"I have written myself almost blind for the last three days, worrying everybody to get a poor young man, who otherwise bears an excellent character, saved from the disgrace and hideous torture of the lash, to which he has exposed himself [by deserting from the army]. I hope to God I shall succeed. He is the son of the man, by me to be ever blessed, who preserved me from being burnt to death in *A Winter's Tale*. The business has cost me a great deal of time; but, if I attain my purpose, I shall be richly paid.

"It is twelve at night; I am tired very much. To-morrow is my last appearance. In a few days I shall go to see my dear girl, Cecilia. How I long to see the darling!

"Oh, how you would have enjoyed my *entrée*, in Constance, last night. I was received really as if it had been my first appearance in the season.

"I have gone about to breakfasts and dinners for this unfortunate young man, till I am quite worn out with them. You know how pleasure, as it is called, fatigues."

Thomas Campbell says that it was the heavy defalcations of payment which Mrs. Siddons and John Kemble had often suffered at Drury Lane, that induced them both to retire from that theatre at the close of the season of 1802. She decided to pay a lengthy professional visit to Ireland. She took a sad farewell of her son, George, who was shortly going out to India ; and she left her daughter in the charge of Mrs. Piozzi.

Sarah Siddons to Mrs. Piozzi.
" *May,* 1802.

" Farewell, my beloved friend ! a long, long farewell ! Oh, such a day as this has been to me. I have been surrounded by my family, and my eyes have dwelt with a foreboding tenderness, too painful, on the venerable face of my dear father, that tells me I shall look upon it no more."—[He died in December.]—" I commit my children to your friendly protection, with a full and perfect reliance on the goodness you have always manifested towards
" Your ever faithful and affectionate
" S. Siddons."

Mrs. Siddons, accompanied by " Patsy " Wilkinson, left her house in Marlborough Street, London, in May, 1802, and proceeded to Ireland, *via* Holyhead, paying a visit on the way to Stratford-on-Avon. Wherever she went she was greeted with the greatest enthusiasm —Dublin, Cork, Belfast—and she admitted that her profits had gone beyond her highest expectations.

Sarah Siddons to Mrs. FitzHugh.
" CORK, *March* 21, 1803.

" MY DEAR FRIEND,
" How shall I sufficiently thank you for all your kindness to me ? You know my heart, and I

K

may spare my words ; for, God knows, my mind is in so distracted a state, that I can hardly write or speak rationally. Oh ! why did not Mr. Siddons tell me when she ”—[their eldest daughter, Sarah]—“ was first taken so ill ? I should then have got clear of this engagement, and what a world of wretchedness and anxiety would have been spared to me ! And yet, good God ! how should I have crossed the sea ? For a fortnight past it has been so dangerous that nothing but wherries have ventured to the Holy Head ; but, yet, I think I should have put myself into one of them, if I could have known that my poor dear girl was so ill.

“ Oh ! tell me all about her. I am almost broken-hearted, though the last accounts tell me that she has been mending for several days. Has she wished for me ? but I know, I feel, that she has. The dear creature used to think it weakness in me, when I told her of the possibility of what might be endured from illness, when that tremendous element divides one from one's family. Would to God I were at her bed-side ! It would be for me then to suffer with resig-nation what I cannot now support with any fortitude. If anything could relieve the misery I feel, it would be that my dear and inestimable Sir Lucas Pepys had her under his care. Pray tell him this, and ask him to write me a word of comfort.

“ Will you believe that I must play to-night, and can you imagine any wretchedness like it in this terrible state of mind ? For a moment I comfort myself by reflecting on the strength of the dear creature's constitution, which has so often rallied, to the astonishment of us all, under similar serious attacks. Then again, when I think of the frail tenure of human existence, my heart fails and sinks into dejection. God bless you! The suspense that distance keeps me in, you may imagine; but it cannot be described.

"Adieu. Your ever affectionate

"S. SIDDONS."

Mrs. Siddons cancelled the rest of her engagement at Cork, and hastened to Dublin, *en route* for England.

Sarah Siddons to Mrs. FitzHugh.

"DUBLIN, *April* 2, 1803.

"I am perfectly astonished, my dear friend, that I have not heard from you, after begging it so earnestly."—[The storm had greatly delayed the mails.]—"Good God! what can be the reason that intelligence must be exhorted, as it were, in circumstances like mine. One would think common benevolence, setting affection quite aside, might have induced some of you to alleviate, as much as possible, such distress as you know I must feel. The last letter from Mr. Siddons stated that she was better. Another letter, from Mr. Montgomery, at Oxford, says that George gave him the same account. Why am I to hear this only from a person at a distance from her, and so ill-informed as the writer must be of the state of her health? Why should not you or Mr. Siddons have told me this ? I cannot account for your silence at all, for you know how to feel. I hope to sail to-night, and to reach London the third day : God knows when that will be. Oh God ! what a home to return to, after all I have been doing ! and what a prospect to the end of my days ! "

Before the arrival in England of Mrs. Siddons, Maria had passed away.

Sarah Siddons to Mrs. FitzHugh.

" BIRCH FARM, CHELTENHAM, *June*, 1803.

" The serenity of the place, the sweet air and scenery of my cottage, and the medicinal effect of the waters, have done some good to my shattered constitution. . . .

" I am unable at times to reconcile myself to my fate. The darling being for whom I mourn is assuredly released from a life of suffering, and numbered among the blessed spirits made perfect. But to be separated for ever, in spite of reason, and in spite of religion, is at times too much for me.

" Give my love to Charles Moore, if you chance to see him. Have you read his beautiful account of my Sally ? It is done with a truth and modesty which has given me the sincerest of all pleasures that I am now allowed to feel, and assures me still more than ever that he who could feel and taste such excellence was worthy of the particular regard she had for him."

Sarah Siddons to a Friend.

" [*? June*, 1803.]

" The testimony of the wisdom of all ages, from the foundation of the world to this day, is childishness and folly, if happiness be anything more than a *name ;* and I am sure our own experience will not enable us to refute the opinion. No, no, it is the inhabitant of a better world. Content, the offspring of moderation, is all we ought to aspire to *here ;* and moderation will be our best and surest guide to that happiness to which she will most assuredly conduct us. If Mr. —— thinks himself unfortunate, let him look on *me,* and be silent. The inscrutable ways of Providence ! Two lovely creatures *gone ;* and another "—[her daughter, Cecilia]—" is just arrived from school, with all the dazzling, frightful sort of beauty that irradiated the countenance of Maria, and makes me shudder when I look at her. I feel myself, like poor Niobe, grasping to her bosom the last and youngest of her children ; and, like her, look every moment for the vengeful arrow of destruction."

Mrs. Siddons was the most circumspect of women in her private life, and there can be no doubt that her strict morality had an influence over some, at least, of her professional sisters, whose manner of life inclined to be less formal. She had admirers innumerable, but she never converted them into lovers. Her happiness she found in her work, her husband, and her children. Also, she was devoted to her parents

and her sisters, though she said sadly, "After I
became famous, none of my sisters loved me as they
did before." Yet she cherished them none the less,
and when Frances Kemble married Francis Twiss, the
author of an *Index to all the Plays of Shakespeare*, she
wrote to a friend : " Yes, my sister is married, and I
have lost one of the sweetest companions in the world.
She has married a most respectable man, though of
small fortune ; and, *I thank God*, that she is off the
stage." One of Mrs. Siddons's sisters, Ann (Mrs.
Curtis), was a thorn in her side. According to Joseph
Knight, Mrs. Curtis " read lectures at Dr. Graham's
Temple of Health, led a discreditable life, attempted
to poison herself in Westminster Abbey, made appeals
to the public, and announced herself everywhere as
the youngest sister of Mrs. Siddons." Ann's endeavours to wring money from her helped to burden
Mrs. Siddons's memory with avarice. Mrs. Siddons
allowed her £20 a year on the condition, it is said, that
she lived one hundred and fifty miles from London.
Under the name of Hutton she wrote novels, and was
known as " Anne of Swansea." In 1783 she published
" *Poems on Miscellaneous Subjects*, by Ann Curtis,
sister of Mrs. Siddons," which she dedicated to the
Duchess of Devonshire.

It has been said that William Brereton fell madly
in love with Mrs. Siddons, and that when she repulsed
him, he endeavoured to commit suicide—but for this
no blame has ever been attached to the actress. She
was, indeed, the last person to be suspected of an
illicit love-affair. Yet, in Ireland in 1802, when she

SARAH SIDDONS
After a portrait by Sir Thomas Lawrence

was forty-seven years of age, she contracted what has been described as " an indiscreet and impulsive friendship " with one Galindo, a fencing-master, which caused the wife, an actress, who regarded herself as much injured, to publish in 1809 : " Mrs. Galindo's Letter to Mrs. Siddons : being a circumstantial detail of Mrs. Siddons's life for seven years ; with several of her letters." To this was added, on the title-page, some lines from Congreve :

> " Dark and unknown betrayer :
> But now the dawn begins, and the slow hand
> Of fate is stretched to draw the veil, and leave
> Thee bare, the naked mark of public view."

Mrs. Galindo, who addressing Mrs. Siddons as " your victim for now seven miserable years," unquestionably was jealous : the only point at issue was what provocation the actress had given her. " In my domestic enjoyment you found me, as you were too well convinced of, in the possession of as great a portion of content as this life can be supposed to have; yet it alone existed in the possession of one blessing, the affection of that object I had sacrificed so much for, yet you with a satanic barbarity resolved to deprive me of this solitary blessing, in spite of all you knew I had suffered, all I must suffer." Thus Mrs. Galindo ; but Mrs. Siddons may be acquitted of " satanic barbarity " : but, it may reasonably be asked, did she lose her head or her heart ?

" About this period," Mrs. Galindo continues, " you proposed to Mr. Jones "—[the manager of the

Dublin theatre]—" to perform *Hamlet*, I now believe for no other purpose than to be taught *fencing* by Mr. Galindo, for, by so doing, you had an excuse to have him constantly with you, to the exclusion of my company, as you said you could not be instructed while any person looked on. You renewed your engagement to play at Cork and Limerick ; we travelled with you in the following manner : Mr. Galindo and I set off early of a morning and stopped at the first stage until you came to breakfast ; you then went into the curricle to Mr. Galindo, and travelled with him the rest of the day, generally arriving, as ours " —[the Galindos' horses in the curricle]—" could not keep up with post-horses, some hours after Miss Wilkinson and myself." This is a fair specimen of the charges. Galindo used to see Mrs. Siddons to her apartments, and return home very late. She contrived to get an engagement for Mr. Galindo in London, and when they were there the husband used to visit the actress at her cottage at Hampstead, and, indeed, he used to stay there " as usual on the sopha." Mrs. Galindo further complained that though Mrs. Siddons's letters were addressed to them both, they were obviously intended only for him. Yet, on the face of them, the letters seem harmless enough ; but Mrs. Galindo was determined to distort everything that had any connection with Mrs. Siddons—the footnotes to the letters now printed are the embittered comments of Mrs. Galindo.

Sarah Siddons to Mrs. Galindo.

" [LONDON, *April* or *May*, 1803.]

" MY DEAR MRS. GALINDO,

" I now again cherish the hope that we may meet again, and enjoy much mutual pleasure in the society of each other. Though *such days as those which are past* we never *can expect to see again.* I have again sounded Mr. Harris on the subject of your return to Covent Garden, and though he cannot give you an engagement for next winter, I think there can be no doubt that I may be able to make one for the ensuing season. Tell me, then, what terms you would have me propose,[1] and do not doubt my zeal. If I do vow a friendship, you know I will perform it to the last article.[2] Write to me immediately, for I will not let the matter cool, if I can avoid it. We talk of you every day, and think of you every moment. Surely, surely, we shall meet again, and though the manner of our intercourse be *different,* yet our *affections* will be unaltered, except that *deprivation* will teach us to estimate even *more highly* what we were near losing for ever.

" Do not let sweet little Johnny[3] or his father forget her who loves them both very affectionately. Oh ! how it would lighten the burden of my sorrows,

---

[1] In my answer, I declined making any. She knew my salary in Dublin ; and, of course, I suppose I must have somewhat more in a London theatre.

[2] I have, I trust, fully stated how truly this *assertion* has been adhered to in respect to me !

[3] My eldest boy, then my only child,

to get you out of the power of that tyrant Jones.[1] . . ."

Sarah Siddons to Mr. Galindo.

" BIRCH FARM, NEAR CHELTENHAM,

" *May* 15, 1803.

" MY KIND FRIEND,

" I enclose you Mr. Harris's letter, which I received about a week ago in answer to one I sent after him to Bath. I must confess the procrastinating of the business (as it was unexpected after the promise given) has caused me a good deal of vexation, but you need not doubt my sincere efforts against it. You do me too much honour, and give me a great deal too much credit in consulting me on the subject of Mr. ———. I am much flattered by your opinion of my ability ; but I am the most incapable person in the world of giving advice upon such a business ; I leave you to the guidance of one who is as competent as any one I know to *all useful knowledge ;* I need not tell you the person I mean is Mrs. Galindo.

" I am extremely sorry to hear she has been ill : remember me kindly to her. I suppose Patsy has given her an account of our habitation here, and the arrangements of our time, not omitting our often repeated wishes, that our friends on the other side of the water could share our homely meals and pleasant walks, and our rejoicing at pretty Julio's health and

---

[1] I do not know why this lady calls Mr. Jones [manager of the Dublin theatre] a tyrant. I never found him so.

beauty.[1] How providential it was, that poor Mrs. Galindo was not in the curricle when he chose to ' cut a caper.'[2]

" Our little cottage is some distance from the town, and perfectly retired; surrounded by fields and hills and groves. The air of this place is peculiarly salubrious. I live out of doors as much as possible, sometimes reading under the haystack in the farmyard, and sometimes musing in the orchard; all which I do without spectators : no observers near, to say I am mad, foolish, or melancholy. Thus I keep the ' noiseless tenor of my way,' and you will be glad to hear this mode of life as well suited to my taste. Rising at six, and going to bed at ten, has brought me to my sleep once more ; the bitterness and anguish of selfish grief begins to subside, and the tender recollections of excellence and virtue gone to the blessed place of their eternal reward are now the sweet, though sad, companions of my lonely walks. I often carry with me that beautiful sonnet, and even suffer myself to hope

' That fancy's radiance, friendship's precious tear,
    Shall soften, shall avert, affliction's gloom.'

" I thank you very much for the epitaph; but cannot help being sorry that Patsy should have imposed so troublesome a task. She is at present my only companion, and is an unspeakable comfort to me. That eulogy, if it may so be called, is a modest

---

[1] One of the curricle horses to which Mrs. Siddons was much attached. I believe she had found herself often indebted to the (happily for her, dumb) docility of those creatures.
[2] A phrase of Mr. Galindo's.

and true picture of that excellent creature's mind and attainments. Oh, what an irreparable loss ! As there is no one who more sincerely wishes you well than I do, your sentiments upon writing it give me the sincerest satisfaction, all share alike the inevitable hour. May it not surprise us unprepared. Think upon it sometimes seriously,[1]

"And forgive the freedom of

"Your obliged friend,

"S. SIDDONS."

Sarah Siddons to Mrs. Galindo.

"CHELTENHAM, *June* 12, 1803.

"MY DEAR MRS. GALINDO,

"I hope long before this you have received the account of my brother's visit to me, and that the assurance of an engagement for three years at five pounds a week has put you[2] all in a more comfortable

---

[1] How kindly anxious this lady was not only for Mr. Galindo's happiness in this world, but in that to come, as will be seen in many of her letters ; but how she purposed *leading* him to *Heaven*, whether by *example* or *precept* is somewhat *doubtful*.

[2] Nothing could be more the reverse in respect to my feelings. Oppressed with a supposed weight of obligation, by the great trouble and exertion Mrs. Siddons said it had cost her to obtain this engagement, and for the first time understanding Mr. Kemble was adverse to it (which had never before been hinted to me), I could not be gratified by obtaining a much more lucrative situation on such terms ; but when I was not to be a gainer of a farthing by the exchange, on the contrary I must forgo many advantages which it was not likely (indeed, possible) I could possess, no words could describe the mortification I felt on reading this letter. My first determination was instantly to refuse it. But alas ! I was not permitted to follow the dictates of my head or my heart. By a blind submission to the *will* of that person to whom I had already sacrificed so much, and an equally blind confidence

frame of mind than Mr. Harris's was likely to produce. I was unwilling to send it, but I thought it right to tell you precisely how the business stood, especially as it was a thing of too much consequence, with respect to your arrangements in the interim.

"This letter is to serve as an answer to Mr. Galindo's,[1] and I sincerely hope I may never receive such another : for, alas ! the pressure of my own affliction has not yet hardened me into an insensibility to the sorrows and mishaps of my friends, my friends too should *know* this ; but I say no more. I most sincerely wish his spirits may be again restored ; he tells me, I have taken too much trouble about this engagement, and that ' happiness is purchased at too dear a price.' I will own, in answer to the first aspersion, that it *has* cost me much and various and very bitter contention ; but I have gained the victory at last, and it depends on the moderation of the wishes and expectations of us all whether the conflict is ended peaceably and honourably.[2] I pray God it may, for to live in a state of contention with a brother I so tenderly love, and a husband[3] with whom I am to

in another, I determined *my ruin* by writing a letter of thanks, from what every feeling of my heart revolted at the acceptance of. Thus was I betrayed by the *two* people in the *world*, in whom I most confided, to follow an *ignis fatuus*, a false hope, which *ultimately* has been my destruction, and that of my helpless infants, by depriving me of the means of preserving or increasing the only dependence they had—the little fortunes and industry of their *deluded mother*.

[1] I know not what caused the remainder of this letter, for though it is addressed to me, it was intended for Mr. Galindo's instruction.

[2] The event has proved how honourable to some of the parties, how destructive to others.

[3] I could never guess what interest Mr. Siddons could have in the business ; but *I suppose* Mr. Galindo *did*.

spend what remains of life, would be more than my subdued spirit and almost broken heart would be able to endure.[1]

" In answer to the second, I can only say that the testimony of the wisdom of all ages, from the foundation of the world to this day, is childishness and folly, if happiness be anything more than a *name*, and I am assured our own experience will not enable us to refute the opinion. No, no; it is the inhabitant of a better world, content, the offspring of moderation, is all we ought to aspire to *here*, and moderation will be our best and surest guide to that happiness to which she will most assuredly conduct us. Forgive this preaching. I have a most sincere and affectionate regard for him, and I wish, for your sake as well as his own, he would endeavour to correct that avidity of imagination that at one time hurries him into what he mistakes for happiness, but which is indeed no other than intoxication—a sort of drunkenness of the mind—and the next moment plunges him into despondency. Indeed, indeed, I wish you would tell him it is my most earnest request that he would, and that, by making this exertion, and in the effects it will produce on your *mutual comforts*, I shall be richly overpaid for all I have done. If he thinks himself unfortunate, let him look on *me*, and be silent—' the

---

[1] This last misery Mr. Siddons did not have long to *endure*, as on my arrival in London, October twelve-month, I found every arrange-ment made between her and Mrs. Siddons for an amicable parting, division of property, etc., etc. He had left London to reside at Bath, and she went to live at Hampstead ; they only occasionally visited each other since I have known them.

inscrutable ways of Providence.' Two lovely creatures
gone, and another [Cecilia] is just arrived from school,
with all the dazzling, frightful sort of beauty that
irradiated the countenance of Maria, and makes me
shudder when I look at her. I feel myself like poor
Niobe, grasping to her bosom the last and youngest of
her children; and, like her, look every moment for
the vengeful arrow of destruction. Alas! my dear
friend! can it be wondered at, that I long for the land
where they are gone to prepare their mother's place?
What have I here? Yet, *here*, even here, I could be
content to linger still in peace and calmness. Content,
is all I wish; but I must again enter into the bustle
of the world. For, the *fame* and *fortune* have given me
all I wish; yet, while my presence and exertions here
may be useful to others, I do not think myself at
liberty to give myself up to my own selfish gratifications. The second great commandment is, love thy
neighbour as thyself; and, in this way, I shall most
probably best make my way to Heaven.[1] Give my
love to dear little Johnny. He will seem pleased at
last, if he has not forgotten to laugh at the name of
Siddons. God bless you all.

> " I am unalterably,
> " Your sincere friend,
> " S. SIDDONS."

In all, Mrs. Galindo prints a score of Mrs. Siddons's
letters. Only two more of these need be given here.

---

[1] How far Mrs. Siddons has fulfilled *this second great commandment*,
let others, not so injured a being as I am, determine for her.

"MANCHESTER,[1] *Sunday*.

" MY DEAR MRS. GALINDO,

"Mr. Galindo has just been here to —— about the plays. He offered me his hand, but I had not duplicity enough to receive it. I need only tell you that he was as violent as usual, and wondered what he had done to offend me. I endeavoured, but in vain, for he had all the talk to himself, to ask him what he thought of telling Mr. ——, that I have *lent* him the money, after I had his solemn promise on account of ——, never to let it be known. I asked him, if he had ever heard me utter a word respecting you, that was not dictated by esteem and cordial good will ; and how he could imagine that if I had an idea that his acquaintance with me would give *you one* moment's uneasiness, that I should not in *that moment* have broken it off. God knows, and he knows too, that I would ;[2] but I always thought you were desirous of keeping it up, as being sure of his at least being in society that could not be disreputable.[3] I tell you all this, *which is all that passed between us at*

---

[1] I received this after Mrs. Siddons and I had parted at Birmingham, on her going to Manchester.

[2] This is a very ridiculous and tardy vindication of what has been constantly practised for upwards of five years, and an appeal to the divine power for the truth ! ! !—to prove the falsehood of which, it is only necessary to request my readers to turn to her fourteenth letter, where she even upbraids me, for having been discontented at Mr. Galindo's spending so much of his time with her when in Dublin.

[3] So far this observation is true. I was well pleased at Mr. Galindo's *visiting* her ; but I did not like his *living with her* (which was often the case) more than at home.

that interview,[1] that you may know from one who never yet told you a falsehood,[2] and as *he* professes to be unable to relate anything accurately, ' the truth, the whole truth, and nothing but the truth,' that you may not be mislead.[3] He was talking so much all the time, that I believe he hardly heard me, when I assured him I was sorry to see him carried away by the violence of his temper—that I harboured no resentment against him—and only hoped he would not hereafter represent me as such a fiend, to turn a man's wife into ridicule of her *husband,*[4] as it was likely to come to the ear of those who are not so deeply impressed with the duty of forgiveness as myself. He went away in a rage, or I might have talked him into a little reason. Adieu, and

" Believe me, dear Mrs. Galindo,

" Your sincere friend,

" S. SIDDONS."

Sarah Siddons to Mr. Galindo.

" Mrs. Siddons's compliments to Mr. Galindo. She declines the favour of any interview, and begs leave

---

[1] Why this sentense is marked so emphatically, I could never comprehend — nor, indeed, the intention of most part of this letter.

[2] All she told, all she professed to me, was falsehood.

[3] There appears a strange confusion of mind in the construction of this sentence, to me totally unintelligible. As it is nothing but *truth*, it is a pity it has not truth's first attribute, clearness.

[4] What she alludes to here, I never could understand. She seems to vindicate herself of what I never heard her accused by *anyone* ; on the contrary, even to Mr. Galindo, I know she always affected to speak well of me.

L

to refer him to Mr. —— for any business he may have
to transact."[1]

So ended this unfortunate affair. Mrs. Galindo
charged Mrs. Siddons with improper connections with
Galindo ; but a careful perusal of the correspondence
and a study of the circumstances establish no more
than grave indiscretion.

Later in the year (1803), Mrs. Siddons and John
Kemble accepted an engagement with Harris for a
season at Covent Garden. The Manager, it has been
recorded, " was immediately and well rewarded by the
profits that accrued from the united talents of the
Kemble and the Siddons, and the addition of sixteen
private boxes to those that were taken by the aris-
tocracy, at a rent of £300 a year each, was a flattering
earnest of what this new connection would achieve."
Mrs. Siddons was tumultuously received when she
appeared on September 27 as Isabella in *The Fatal
Marriage*, and again on October 6 when she played
Lady Randolph to the Douglas of her son Henry, and
the Old Norval of Kemble. As proof of her amazing
vitality, it may be stated that between September,
1803, and May, 1804, she performed sixty times—
Isabella five times, Mrs. Haller three times, Elvira

---

[1] Upon Mr. Galindo's requesting to see her to explain his situation
with Mr. M'Cready ; yet, though she here refers him to her agent, though
he waited on her to explain every circumstance, and afterwards wrote
to him to know Mrs. Siddons's determination, neither from this person
nor her, has he been able to obtain any answer to his offer of making
over to Mrs. Siddons the half of the annuity he receives from Mr.
M'Cready, in liquidation of her debt to her, and she knows but too
well, he has no other means of paying her.

twelve times, Mrs. Beverley five times, Calesta four times, Belvidera six times, Isabella in *Measure for Measure* twice, Lady Macbeth seven times, Hermione in *The Distressed Mother* twice, Desdemona six times, Zara in *The Mourning Bride* twice, Constance twice, Lady Randolph, Jane Shore, Queen Mary, *Grecian Daughter* once each. During the season 1804–5, however, she only played twice. She gave ill-health as the explanation ; but probably the real reason was the appearance of the infant phenomenon, Master Betty, with whom her dignity would not allow her to act. When Lord Abercorn, with extraordinary tactlessness, said to her that Betty would eclipse everything which had been called acting in England, " My Lord," she answered, " he is a very clever, pretty boy, but nothing more."

In the summer of 1805 Mrs. Siddons played at Edinburgh and Dublin, and later in the year she acted thirty-nine times at Covent Garden.

Sarah Siddons to a Friend.

" LIVERPOOL, *July* 15, 1807.

" The houses are tolerably good. I can't expect to be followed like that great genius, Master Betty, you know ; but I hope to put about £1000 into my pocket this summer. 'Tis better to work hard for a short time and have done with it. If I can but add £300 a year to my present income, I shall be perfectly well provided for ; and I am resolved, when that is accomplished, to make no more positive engagements in summer. I trust that God, in His great mercy, will enable me to do it; and then, oh, how lazy, and saucy, and happy I will be. You will have something to do, I can tell you, my dear, to keep me in order."

On September 20, 1808, Covent Garden was destroyed by fire.

Sarah Siddons to Lady Harcourt.

"*September*, 1808.

"MY DEAR LADY HARCOURT,

"As yet, I have had neither recollection, nor time, to think of anything except the tremendous devastation and its afflicting consequences. My poor brother bears it most nobly, with manly firmness, hope, and even cheerful resignation. As for me, I now think only of the mercy which was vouchsafed us in his not hearing of the fire till the whole structure was devoured, so that the lives of both my brothers, which would have been risked in the efforts they would have exerted, perhaps at the expense of limbs and life, are safe. God be praised.

"I myself was in the house till near twelve o'clock. Mr. Brandon"—[secretary and treasurer of Covent Garden theatre]—"and the watchman saw all safe at near one, and it is as true as it is strange that not a fragment of the whole structure was discoverable at six, at which time my brother first heard of it, and he declared that at that time it was so completely destroyed that you could not have known a building had stood there.

" The losses of scenery, dresses, etc., are, as you may imagine, irreparable. I have lost everything, all my jewels and lace, which I have been collecting for thirty years, and which I could not purchase again, for they were all really fine and curious. I had a point veil which had been a toilette of the poor Queen of France, near five yards long, and which could not have been bought for anything like so little as a thousand pounds, destroyed, with dresses of my own, of great value for costume. In short, everything I had in the world of stage ornament is gone, and not one vestige left of all that has cost me so much time and money to collect.

" We are to act at the Opera, and next Monday I shall attempt the character of Lady Randolph there. My poor dear brother has to begin the world again. Mrs. Kemble bears it like an angel. Of course, I am with them every moment that I can. It is a glorious feeling to see how many noble and friendly attentions have been shown to him on this occasion.

" Lord Guilford and Lord Mountjoy have offered to advance him any sum of money they can raise by any means. My head is confused. I scarce know what I write ; but you, my dear Lady Harcourt, will have the goodness to excuse any incoherence under these circumstances. The Prince, too, has been so good and gracious. Everybody is good and kind, and, please God, we shall still do well. Adieu ! "

The Covent Garden company transferred itself to the Haymarket Theatre, and there, between September, 1808, and May, 1809, Mrs. Siddons performed forty times. In the summer of the latter year she went again to Scotland, where she met Henry Erskine, Walter Scott, and James Ballantyne. " At the period of which I am now writing," Lockhart says, " Scott's principal theatrical intimacy was with John Philip Kemble and his sister, Mrs. Siddons, both of whom he appears to have often met at Lord Abercorn's villa near Stanmore during his spring visits to London after the first establishment of his poetical character. . . . John Kemble's most familiar table-talk often flowed into blank verse : and so indeed did his sister's. Scott, who was a capital mimic, often repeated her tragic exclamation to a foot-boy during a dinner :

' You've brought me water, boy—I asked for beer.'

Another time, dining with the Provost of Edinburgh, she ejaculated, in answer to her host's apology for his *pièce de résistance :*

' Beef cannot be too salt for me, my Lord.' "

Covent Garden Theatre reopened on September 18, 1809, with *Macbeth,* the Thane being played by Kemble, and Lady Macbeth by Mrs. Siddons. This was to be followed by a musical entertainment, *The Quaker.* For the new building, owing to the cost of the erection, it had been found necessary slightly to alter the galleries and somewhat to increase the prices. The house was packed ; the National Anthem sung—and then pandemonium broke out when Kemble came forward to recite a poetical address on the opening of the building. This lasted through-

out the performance, with the result that the play
was given in dumb show. The disturbances went on
for nights, in spite of the arrest of the ringleaders.
" There was a strange mixture of whimsicality and
distressing circumstances exhibited all through the
riot," Thomas John Didbin has recalled. " When
the performers entered, they were greeted with
applause, to indicate that what would follow was not
meant personally to them; but the instant they
attempted to speak, ' Off ! Off ! ' overpowering hisses,
appalling hoots, and the ' O.P. Dance ' commenced,
in which the whole audience joined. The dance was
performed with deliberate and ludicrous gravity, each
person pronouncing the letters ' O.P. ' as loud as he
could, and accompanying the pronunciation of each
with a beat, or blow on the floor or seat beneath him
with his feet, a stick, or a bludgeon, and as the
numerous performers kept in strict time and unison
with each other, it was one of the most whimsically
tantalising banters or torments that could be conceived. Numerous placards were exhibited in all
parts of the theatre, some of them very offensive,
others ludicrous."

The " O.P. riots " excluded Mrs. Siddons from the
stage for the greater part of the season.

Sarah Siddons to Mrs. FitzHugh.

" WESTBOURNE FARM, *December* 2, 1809.

" I am quite vexed, my dear, with Miss L., for
giving you such an account of me. My appearance of

illness was occasioned entirely by an agitating visit
that morning from poor Mr. John Kemble, on account
of the giving up of the private boxes, which, I fear,
must be at last complied with. Surely nothing ever
equalled the domineering of the mob in these days.
It is to me inconceivable how the public at large sub-
mits to be thus dictated to, against their better judgment, by a handful of imperious and intoxicated men.
In the meantime, what can the poor proprietors do,
but yield to overwelming necessity ?

" Could I once feel that my poor brother's anxiety
about the Theatre was at an end, I should be, marvellous to say, as well as ever I was in my life. But
only conceive what a state he must have been in,
however good a face he might put upon the business,
for upwards of three months ; and think what his
poor wife and I must have suffered, when, for weeks
together, such were the outrages committed on his
house and otherwise, that I trembled for even his
personal safety ; she, poor soul, living with ladder at
her window, in order to make her escape through the
garden, in case of an attack. Mrs. Kemble tells me
his nerves are much shaken. What a time it has been
with us all, beginning with fire, and continued with
fury. Yet sweet sometimes are the uses of adversity.
They not only strengthen family affection, but teach
us all to walk humbly with our God."

Further trouble ensued—or, at least, there was a
continuation of the trouble—when Kemble engaged
the famous foreign singer, Madam Catalini. Mr. Saxe

Wyndham has printed some lines about her, under the style of " The Cat," that appeared at the time in the *Chronicle*.

" This is the house that Jack built.
  These are the boxes let to the great that visit the house, etc.
  These are the pigeon-holes over the boxes let to the great, etc.
  This is the Cat engaged to squall to the poor in the pigeon-holes, etc.
  This is John Bull with a bugle-horn that hissed the Cat, etc.
  This is the thief-taker, shaven and shorn, that took up John Bull, etc.
  This is the Manager full of scorn, who raised the prices to the people forlorn,
  And directed the thief-taker, shaven and shorn,
  To take up John Bull with his bugle-horn,
  Who hissed the Cat engaged to squall to the poor in the pigeon-holes over the boxes let to the great that visit the house that Jack built."

In the end Kemble had to consent to the demolition of the boxes, and peace was restored.

Mrs. Siddons, having now amassed a sufficient competence, decided to retire while her powers were still undiminished. During the season of 1811–12 she performed at Covent Garden fifty-seven times. She took her farewell of the stage, in the part of Lady Macbeth, on June 29, 1812.

Mrs. Siddons now lived quietly at Westbourne Farm, " Patsy " Wilkinson still her constant company ; but she moved much in society, and greatly enjoyed her well-earned repose after the strenuous life she had led for so long. She survived until June 15, 1831, and was buried with much pomp and circumstance, in what was then called the New Ground

of Paddington Church. The grave bears the simple
inscription :

Sacred to the Memory of

SARAH SIDDONS,

Who departed this life, June 8, 1831,
in her 76th year.

" Blessed are the dead who die in the Lord "

MARY ANNE ("PERDITA") ROBINSON
(*née* DARBY)
1758–1800

MARY ANNE ("PERDITA")
ROBINSON (*née* DARBY)
1758–1800

THE fame of Mary Anne Robinson is almost entirely based upon the fact that on December 3, 1778, when playing Perdita in Garrick's adaptation of *A Winter's Tale*, at Drury Lane, the Prince of Wales was attracted by her beauty and figure. When the point is made against George that he behaved badly to the lady, it is fair to recall the fact that he was sixteen years of age, and had been as far as possible kept in seclusion by the King, whereas " Perdita," as henceforth she was generally called, was four years his senior, was a married woman, and was used to the amorous rough and tumble of the stage and the patrons, or would-be patrons of theatrical " stars," great and small.

Mary Anne Robinson, who was born on November 27, 1758, at College Green, Bristol, was of Irish descent. The name of her father's family was originally Macdermott, but it had been changed by one of her ancestors to Darby. Through her mother, whose maiden name was Seys, she claimed descent from Locke. There were several children of the marriage : John, who went to Leghorn, established himself as a merchant, and survived until 1790 ;

Elizabeth, who died in infancy ; Mary Anne; William, who only lived six years ; and George, who went out and joined his brother John in business. Mary Anne has written down her earliest impressions :

"All the offspring of my parents were, in their infancy, uncommonly handsome, excepting myself. The boys were fair and lusty, with auburn hair, light blue eyes, and countenances peculiarly animated and lovely. I was swarthy ; my eyes were singularly large in proportion to my face, which was small and round, exhibiting features peculiarly marked with most pensive and melancholy cast.

"The great difference betwixt my brothers and myself, in point of personal beauty, tended much to endear me to my parents, particularly to my father, whom I strongly resembled. The early propensities of my life were tinctured with romantic and singular characteristics ; some of which I shall here mention, as proofs that the mind is never to be diverted from its original bent ; and that every event of my life has more or less been marked by the progressive evils of a too acute sensibility.

"The nursery in which I passed my hours of infancy was so near the great aisle of the Minster, that the organ, which re-echoed its deep tones, accompanied by the chaunting of the choristers, was distinctly heard both at morning and evening service. I remember with what pleasure I used to listen, and how much I was delighted whenever I was permitted to sit on the winding-steps which led from the aisle to the cloisters.

MARY ANNE (" PERDITA ") ROBINSON
After a portrait by Englehart

I can at this moment recall to memory the sensations I then experienced ; the tones that seemed to thrill through my heart, the longing which I felt to unite my feeble voice to the full anthem, and the awful, though sublime impression which the church service never failed to make upon my feelings. While my brothers were playing on the green before the Minster, the servant who attended us has often, by my earnest entreaties, suffered me to remain beneath the great eagle which stood in the centre of the aisle, to support the book from which the clergyman read the lessons of the day ; and nothing could keep me away, even in the coldest seasons, but the stern looks of an old man, whom I named Black John from the colour of his beard and complexion, and whose occupations within the sacred precincts were those of a bell-ringer and sexton."

Mary Anne was precocious, and at an unusually early age learnt to read. Before she was seven she could repeat Pope's " Lines to an Unfortunate Lady " and Mason's " Elegy on the Death of the Countess of Coventry," and other poems. Her education began early. " I had then been attended two years by various masters," she says. " Mr. Edmund Broadrip taught me music, my father presented me with one of Kirkman's finest harpsichords, as an encitement to emulation. The only melody which pleased me was that of the mournful and touching kind. Two of my earliest favourites were the celebrated ballad by Gay, beginning, ' 'Twas when the sea was roaring,' and the simple pathetic stanzas of the ' The Heavy Hours,' by the poet Lord Lyttelton. These, though Nature had given me but little voice, I could at seven years of age sing so pathetically, that my mother, to the latest hour of her life, never could bear to hear the latter of them repeated. They reminded her of sorrows, in which I have since painfully learned to sympathise." Presently, she went to a school at Bristol, kept by the sisters of Hannah More. Among the pupils were two daughters of William Powell, so it came about that when the actor was taking a benefit, the whole school attended the theatre, and " Perdita " saw her first dramatic representation.

Darby, who had been captain of a whaler, had settled as a merchant at Bristol, and was a prosperous man. Anxious, however, to increase his fortune, he interested himself in a scheme to establish a whale fishery on the coast of Labrador, employing Esquimaux labour. The scheme was blessed by the Earl of Hillsborough, Sir Hugh Palliser, the Earl of Bristol, the Earl of Chatham, and Lord Northington (Mary Anne's godfather), who seemed to think that the whale fishery of Labrador might be as productive as that of Greenland. The only trouble was, that it was absolutely necessary, if the project was to have a fair chance of success, for Darby to go to America and stay there for at least two years. In vain his wife, who felt an invincible antipathy to the sea, tried to dissuade him, so she stayed in England with her children. At first letters came as often as was possible, then the intervals were longer, at length a silence of

MARY ANNE ("PERDITA") ROBINSON

After a portrait by Gainsborough

months. Presently Mrs. Darby learnt that the cause
of the silence was a new attachment. And then,
three years after his departure, he returned. "I was
not then quite ten years old, though so tall and
formed in my person that I might have passed for
twelve or thirteen," "Perdita" writes. "On our
arrival in London we repaired to my father's lodgings
in Spring Gardens. He received us, after three years'
absence, with a mixture of pain and pleasure; he
embraced us with tears, and his voice was scarcely
articulate. My mother's agitation was indescribable;
she received a cold embrace at their meeting—it was
the last she ever received from her alienated husband."
Darby announced that he had only come back on
business; that he was going back to America; and
that he would pay for his wife's board in any private
and respectable family. Soon after the arrival of the
family in London, Mary Anne was sent to a school at
Chelsea. "The mistress of this seminary was perhaps
one of the most extraordinary women that ever graced,
or disgraced, society; her name was Meribah Lorrington," she recalls. "She was the most extensively
accomplished female that I ever remember to have
met with; her mental powers were no less capable
of cultivation than superiorly cultivated. Her father,
whose name was Hull, had from her infancy been the
master of an academy at Earl's Court, near Fulham;
and early after his marriage, losing his wife, he
resolved on giving his daughter a masculine education. Meribah was early instructed in all the modern
accomplishments, as well as in classical knowledge.

M

She was mistress of the Latin, French, and Italian
languages, she was said to be a perfect arithmetician
and astronomer, and possessed the art of painting on
silk to a degree of exquisite perfection. But, alas !
with all these advantages she was addicted to one
vice, which at times so completely absorbed her facul-
ties as to deprive her of every power, either mental
or corporeal. Thus, daily and hourly, her superior
acquirements, her enlightened understanding, yielded
to the intemperance of her ruling infatuation, and
every power of reflection seemed lost in the unfeminine
propensity. All that I ever learned I acquired from
this extraordinary woman. In those hours when her
senses were not intoxicated she would delight in the
task of instructing me. She had only five or six pupils,
and it was my lot to be her particular favourite. She
always, out of school, called me her little friend, and
made no scruple of conversing with me (sometimes
half the night, for I slept in her chamber) on domestic
and confidential affairs. I felt for her a very sincere
affection, and I listened with peculiar attention to
all the lessons she inculcated. Once I recollect her
mentioning the particular failing which disgraced so
intelligent a being : she pleaded, in excuse of it, the
immitigable regret of a widowed heart, and with com-
punction declared that she flew to intoxication as the
only refuge from the pang of prevailing sorrow. I
continued more than twelve months under the care
of Mrs. Lorrington, during which period my mother
boarded in a clergyman's family at Chelsea. I applied
rigidly to study, and acquired a taste for books, which

has never, from that time, deserted me. Mrs. Lorrington frequently read to me after school hours, and I to her: I sometimes indulged my fancy in writing verses or composing rebuses, and my governess never failed to applaud the juvenile compositions I presented to her. Some of them, which I preserved and printed in a small volume shortly after my marriage, were written when I was between twelve and thirteen years of age; but as love was the theme of my poetical phantasies, I never showed them to my mother till I was about to publish them." The tragic end of Mrs. Lorrington is related by her pupil: " Shortly after my mother had established herself at Chelsea, on a summer's evening, as I was sitting at the window, I heard a deep sigh, or rather a groan of anguish, which suddenly attracted my attention. The night was approaching rapidly, and I looked towards the gate before the house, where I observed a woman evidently labouring under excessive affliction; I instantly descended and approached her. She, bursting into tears, asked whether I did not know her. Her dress was torn and filthy, she was almost naked, and an old bonnet, which nearly hid her face, so completely disfigured her features that I had not the smallest idea of the person who was then almost sinking before me. I gave her a small sum of money, and inquired the cause of her apparent agony. She took my hand and pressed it to her lips. ' Sweet girl,' said she, ' you are still the angel I ever knew you ! ' I was astonished. She raised her bonnet; her fine dark eyes met mine. It was Mrs. Lorrington. I led her into the house ; my mother was not at home. I took her to my chamber, and with the assistance of a lady who was our French teacher, I clothed and comforted her. She refused to say how she came to be in so deplorable a situation, and took her leave. It was in vain that I entreated, that I conjured her to let me know where I might send to her. She refused to give me her address, but promised that in a few days she would call on me again. It is impossible to describe the wretched appearance of this accomplished woman. The failing to which she had now yielded, as to a monster that would destroy her, was evident at the moment when she was speaking to me. I saw no more of her : but to my infinite regret was informed some years after that she had died, the martyr of a premature decay, brought on by the indulgence of her propensity to intoxication—in the workhouse of Chelsea."

Owing to " pecuniary derangement " Mrs. Lorrington gave up her school and Mary Anne went to a boarding-school at Battersea, until her father ceased to send supplies. Then Mrs. Darby set up a scholastic establishment at Little Chelsea, and Mary Anne, at the age of fourteen, became a junior mistress. Her husband, however, when he heard of this, peremptorily ordered his wife to close the school. This she did, and Mary Anne was sent to be " finished " at Oxford House, Marylebone, where she employed every leisure moment in writing verse : she even essayed a tragedy. This was, if she had known it, the turning-point of her life, for the dancing-master at Oxford House was Hussey, the ballet-master at Covent

Garden Theatre. Through him, or another, Mary met Arthur Murphy and David Garrick. Garrick took a fancy to the beautiful girl, and told her if she liked to go on the stage—he had heard her recite—she should make her début as Cordelia to his Lear. Mrs. Darby, however, vetoed the idea, dreading the perils and the temptations of the theatre.

Mary Anne's first proposal of marriage had been made by a naval officer when she was only thirteen—from her appearance, he thought she was three years older. Now numerous admirers, honourable and otherwise, came upon the scene. " My person improved daily," she says ; " yet a sort of dignified air, which from a child I had acquired, effectually shielded me from the attacks of impertinence and curiosity." Then, she met Thomas Robinson, an articled clerk, who gave out that he was well-to-do and had expectations from a wealthy uncle He fell in love, and won the consent of Mrs. Darby to the marriage by promising that she should live with them. The banns were put up at St. Martin's-in-the-Field, and they were married on April 12, 1774. At the last moment, Robinson, urging various reasons, begged that the marriage should be kept secret : it presently transpired that he was not the nephew and heir, but the illegitimate son, of the man from whom he expected a handsome fortune. Soon Mrs. Robinson was honoured with the attentions, among others, of " the bad " Lord Lyttelton and George Robert Fitzgerald. " Lord Lyttelton, who was perhaps the most accomplished libertine that any age or country has produced, with considerable artifice inquired after Mr. Robinson, professed his earnest desire to cultivate his acquaintance, and on the following day sent him a card of invitation," the girl-wife writes. " Lyttleton was an adept in the artifices of fashionable intrigue : he plainly perceived that both Mr. Robinson and myself were uninitiated in its mysteries : he knew that to undermine a wife's honour he must become master of the husband's confidence, and Mr. Robinson was too much pleased with the society of a man whose wit was only equalled by his profligacy to shrink from such an association.

" Fortunately for me, Lord Lyttelton was uniformly my aversion. His manners were overbearingly insolent, his language licentious, and his person slovenly even to a degree that was disgusting. Mr. Robinson was in every respect the reverse of his companion : he was unassuming, neat, and delicate in his conversation. I had not a wish to descend from the propriety of wedded life, and I abhorred, decidedly abhorred, the acquaintance of Lord Lyttelton.

" Of those who frequented our house, Lord Lyttelton was most decidedly my abhorrence ; I knew that he frequently led my husband from the paths of domestic confidence to the haunts of profligate debasement. Towards me his lordship affected great indifference ; he has even in my presence declared that no woman under thirty years of age was worth admiring ; that even the antiquity of forty was far preferable to the insipidity of sixteen ; and he generally concluded his observations by hoping he had not made ' the *pretty child* angry.' " Robinson neglected his wife, and was unfaithful to her—as Lyttelton, in pursuit of her, told her—but they lived together in Hatton Gardens, and entertained on a considerable scale.

Soon after Mary Anne was brought to bed of a daughter, the end came. Robinson was arrested at the suit of his creditors, whose claims amounted to twelve hundred pounds. She shared his confinement in the King's Bench prison for ten months, beguiling the weary hours by writing poems. She, through her brother, sent the manuscript of her verses to the Duchess of Devonshire, who invited her to call, and gave her patronage to a volume, which appeared in 1775.

When Robinson was released, husband and wife found themselves confronted with the problem of how to live. His father refused to come to the rescue, her mother could not ; he had not completed his articles, and could not follow his profession ; the earnings of her pen could not support them. By a happy chance, Mary met William Brereton, the actor, whose acquaintance she had made at Drury Lane, and he suggested that she should go on the stage. He brought Sheridan to see her, and made her recite. Garrick was informed, and again interested himself in the girl. He, Sheridan, Brereton, and her husband assembled in the Greenroom of Drury Lane Theatre, where she recited the principal scenes of Juliet—in which character it was decided that she should make her début. Garrick, who had retired, attended rehearsals, coached her indefatigably.

Mary's first appearance, which was on December 10, 1776, established her in the good graces of the

audience. In the following February she played
Statera in *Alexander the Great*, and created Armanda
in *A Trip to Scarborough*. This was Sheridan's adaptation of Vanbrugh's *The Relapse*, and the house, who
expected a new play, hooted. The young, inexperi-
enced actress was naturally much perturbed, until the
Duke of Cumberland, from the stage-box, reassured
her by calling out, " It is not you, but the play, they
hiss."

Unfortunately for Mary Anne, there was another
young star on the horizon, the beautiful Elizabeth
Farren, whose charms have been immortalised by
Zoffany and Sir Thomas Lawrence. At the age of
fifteen she had played at Liverpool Rosetta in *Love
in a Village*, and then the famous part of Mrs. Townly
in *The Provoked Husband*. Her Liverpool manager,
Younger, was so struck by her ability that he introduced her to Colman, under whose auspices she made
her first appearance in London, at the Haymarket, as
Miss Hardcastle, on June 9, 1777. She at once won
favour, and was speedily recognised as a leading
London actress and a worthy successor to the great
Mrs. Abington. Of course, her early theatrical training gave her the *pas* of Mary Anne Robinson, whenever it was a question of casting one or other for a
part : a fact which Mary Anne much resented.

In the summer of 1778 Mary Anne quarrelled with
the Haymarket management. She had been promised
the part of Nancy Lovel in *The Suicide*, but Miss Farren
was preferred. " I wrote to Mr. Colman, requesting
an explanation," she says. " He replied, that he had

ELIZABETH FARREN, COUNTESS OF DERBY

After the pastel sketch by Ozias Humphreys

promised the part to Miss Farren, who had then performed one or two seasons at the Haymarket theatre.
I felt myself insulted. I insisted on Mr. Colman's
fulfilling his engagement, or on giving me liberty to
quit London : the latter he refused. I demanded to
perform the part of Nancy Lovel. Mr. Colman was
too partial to Miss Farren to hazard offending her.
I refused to play till I had this first character, as by
agreement, restored to me ; and the summer passed
without my once performing, though my salary was
paid weekly and regularly." During the following
winter, however, she performed—with increasing
approbation, she assures us—many characters. Her
success was probably largely due to her looks. Genest
says, " She was a most beautiful woman, with a very
good breeches figure."

The King commanded a performance of the *Winter's
Tale* on December 3, 1778, at Drury Lane. Mary
Anne played Perdita. She had not before performed
before his Majesty, and was very excited, and felt " a
strange degree of alarm." To reassure her, " Gentleman " Smith, who had been cast for Leontes, said to
her, " By Jove, Mrs. Robinson, you will make a conquest of the Prince, for to-night you look handsomer
than ever." His Royal Highness came, attended by
Lord Malden (George Capel Coningsby, afterwards
fifth Earl of Essex), and General Lake. " I hurried
through the first scene, not without much embarrassment, owing to the fixed attention with which the
Prince of Wales honoured me. Indeed, some flattering remarks which were made by his royal highness

met my ear as I stood near his box, and I was overwhelmed with confusion.

"The Prince's particular attention was observed
by everyone, and I was again rallied at the end of
the play. On the last curtsey, the royal family con-
descendingly returned a bow to the performers ; but
the Prince of Wales, and with a look that I never shall
forget, he gently inclined his head a second time ; I
felt the compliment, and blushed my gratitude.

"During the entertainment Lord Malden never
ceased conversing with me ; he was young, pleasing,
and perfectly accomplished. He remarked the particular attention which the Prince had bestowed on
my performance ; said a thousand civil things ; and
detained me in conversation till the evening's performance was concluded.

"I was now going to my chair, which waited, when
I met the royal family crossing the stage. I was again
honoured with a very marked and low bow from the
Prince of Wales. On my return home, I had a party
to supper ; and the whole conversation centred in
encomiums on the person, graces, and amiable
manners of the illustrious heir-apparent." "Gentleman" Smith had been an unconscious prophet. Mary
Anne had made a conquest of this lad of sixteen. A
few days after the performance Lord Malden called
on the lady, and "I received him rather awkwardly.
But his lordship's embarrassment far exceeded mine :
he attempted to speak—hesitated, apologised ; I
know not why. He hoped I would pardon him ; that

I would not mention something he had to communicate; that I would consider the peculiar delicacy of his situation, and then act as I thought proper. I could not comprehend his meaning, and therefore requested that he would be explicit.

" After some moments of evident rumination, he tremblingly drew a small letter from his pocket. I took it, and knew not what to say. It was addressed to PERDITA. I smiled, I believe rather sarcastically, and opened the *billet*. It contained only a few words, but those expressive of more than common civility : they were signed FLORIZEL.

" ' Well, my lord, and what does this mean ? ' said I, half angry.

" ' Can you not guess the writer ? ' said Lord Malden.

" ' Perhaps yourself, my lord,' cried I gravely.

" ' Upon my honour, no,' said the viscount. 'I should not have dared so to address you on so short an acquaintance.

" I pressed him to tell me from whom the letter came. He again hesitated ; he seemed confused, and sorry that he had undertaken to deliver it. ' I hope that I shall not forfeit your good opinion,' said he, ' but ——'

" ' But what, my lord ? '

" ' I could not refuse—for the letter is from the Prince of Wales.'

" I was astonished ; I confess that I was agitated ; but I was also somewhat sceptical as to the truth of Lord Malden's assertion. I returned a formal and a doubtful answer, and his lordship shortly after took his leave."

When the Prince saw her at the theatre he ogled her outrageously. He sent her his portrait in miniature, and put in the case a small heart cut in paper, on one side of which was written " Je ne change qu' en mourant," and on the other, " Unalterable to my Perdita through life." They corresponded for months before they met. In these letters Mary Anne " always offered his Royal Highness "the best advice in my power," she says, " I disclaimed every sordid and interested thought; I recommended to him to be patient till he should become his own master; to wait till he knew more of my mind and manners before he engaged in a public attachment to me; and, above all, to do nothing that might incur the displeasure of his Royal Highness's family. I entreated him to recollect that he was young, and led on by the impetuosity of passion; that should I consent to quit my profession and my husband, I should be thrown entirely on his mercy. I strongly pictured the temptations to which beauty would expose him; the many arts that would be practised to undermine me in his affections; the public abuse which calumny and envy would heap upon me; and the misery I should suffer if after I had given him every proof of confidence he should change in his sentiments towards me. To all this I received repeated assurances of inviolable affection; and I most firmly believe that his Royal Highness meant what he professed; indeed his soul was too ingenuous, his mind too liberal, and his heart too susceptible to deceive premeditatedly, or to harbour even for a moment the idea of deliberate deception."

The end was a foregone conclusion. Her husband, according to her, was openly unfaithful. Her vanity was immense, and the adulation of royalty tickled it much. A meeting was arranged at Kew, the Prince being accompanied by his brother, Frederick Augustus, afterwards Duke of York. The matter was clinched by his Royal Highness giving her a bond for £20,000, payable when he came of age. "This paper was signed by the Prince, and sealed with the royal arms. It was expressed in terms so liberal, so voluntary, so marked by true affection, that I had scarcely power to read it. My tears, excited by the most agonising conflicts, obscured the letters, and nearly blotted out those sentiments, which will be impressed upon my mind till the latest period of my existence. Still, I felt shocked and mortified at the indelicate idea of entering into any pecuniary engagements with a prince, on whose establishment I relied for the enjoyment of all that would render life desirable. I was surprised at receiving it; the idea of interest had never entered my mind : secure in the possession of his heart, I had in that delightful certainty counted all my future treasure. I had refused many splendid gifts which his Royal Highness had proposed ordering for me at Grey's and other jewellers. The Prince presented to me a few trifling ornaments, in the whole their value not exceeding one hundred guineas. Even these on our separation I returned to his Royal Highness through the hands of General Lake."

Attention may, perhaps, be called to the fact—as throwing light on the character of the lady—that "on separation" she returned the "few trifling ornaments"; in the whole their value not exceeding one hundred guineas; but did not surrender the bond for twenty thousand pounds! What independence and dignity!

The intimacy was more or less concealed until 1781, when the Prince was provided with an establishment of his own at Buckingham House, when he was henceforth his own master. He now drove openly with her in a carriage for which he had paid—or, more probably, owed—nine hundred guineas. "She was always magnificently dressed," a contemporary has described her. "To day, she was a *paysanne*, with her straw hat tied at the back of her head; yesterday, she perhaps had been the dressed *belle* of Hyde Park, trimmed, powdered, patched, painted to the utmost power of rouge and white lead; to-morrow she would be the cravated Amazon of the riding-house; but be she what she might, the hats of the fashionable promenaders swept the ground as she passed."

The Prince of Wales soon tired of his charmer, and had it made known to her that their intimacy must cease; that, in fact, he did not want to see her again, and would not do so. The shock to the lady was overwhelming. She wrote to him; he ignored her letters. She drove to Windsor; he declined to receive her. At last, through the intercession of Lord Malden, who was now making love to her on his own account, he granted her an interview. "He accosted me with every appearance of tender attachment, declaring that he had never for one moment ceased to love me

—but, that I had many concealed enemies, who were exerting every effort to undermine me. We passed some hours in the most friendly and delightful conversation, and I began to flatter myself that all our differences were adjusted. But words cannot express my surprise and chagrin, when, on meeting his Royal Highness the *very next day*, in Hyde Park, he turned his head to avoid seeing me, and even affected *not to know me !* "

Mary Anne's condition was now parlous. She had retired from the stage on May 31, 1780, and did not feel, now that she was so notorious, that she might venture to return. She had lived extravagantly in Cork Street, Burlington Gardens, and was heavily in debt, it is said to the extent of £7,000—but there was always the bond for £20,000. When the time came for payment, however, the Prince declined to honour it. In despair, she threatened to publish his Royal Highness's letters, unless they were purchased for a large sum. The matter came to the knowledge of the King, who took the threat very seriously. He felt himself constrained at almost any cost to avert a scandal that would be so damaging to the Heir-apparent. " I am sorry to be obliged to open a subject to Lord North that has long given me much pain, but I can rather do it on paper than in conversation : it is a subject of which I know he is not ignorant," he wrote to Lord North on August 28, 1781. " My eldest son last year got into a very improper connection with an actress and woman of indifferent character through the *friendly* assistance of Lord Malden ; a multitude of letters passed, which she has threatened to publish, unless he, in short, bought of her. He had made her very foolish promises, which, undoubtedly, by her conduct to him, she entirely cancelled. I have thought it right to authorise the getting them from her, and have employed Lieutenant-Colonel Hotham, on whose discretion I could depend, to manage this business. He has now brought it to a conclusion, and has her consent to get these letters on her receiving five thousand pounds, undoubtedly an enormous sum; but I wish to get my son out of this shameful scrape. I desire you will therefore see Lieutenant-Colonel Hotham and settle this with him. I am happy at being able to say that I never was personally engaged in such a transaction, which perhaps makes me feel this the stronger."

Eventually the affair of the adjustment of the bond was placed in the hands of Charles James Fox, and, by his management, it was commuted to an official pension of five hundred a year, one half of which was to be continued to Mary Anne's daughter for life. This was entered on the records as given in consideration of the " resignation of a lucrative profession at the particular request of his Royal Highness the Prince of Wales." It was generally supposed that Fox, whom she met first in the Green-room of Drury Lane, succeeded the Prince as her lover. "*Pour se désen-nuyer*, Fox lives with Mrs. Robinson, goes to Sadler's Wells with her, and is all day figuring away with her," Horace Walpole mentioned in 1782; and this intimacy gave rise to a *bon mot* of George Selwyn:

" Who should the Man of the People live with but the Woman of the People ? " Mary Anne thought the settlement stingy. "Have I not reason to be disgusted when I see the Prince to whom I ought to look for better service lavishing favours on unworthy objects, gratifying the avarice of ignorance and dulness," she asked; "while, I, who sacrificed reputation, an advantageous profession, friends, patronage, the brilliant hours of youth, and the conscious delight of correct conduct, am condemned to the scanty pittance bestowed on every indifferent page who holds up the ermined trains of ceremony."

Mary Anne, about 1783, went to Paris with her daughter, and there attracted much attention, and received overtures from the Duke of Orleans, which she is supposed to have rejected. While crossing the Channel she wrote the following lines :

STANZAS

Written between Dover and Calais, July 20th, 1792.

Bounding billow, cease thy motion,
    Bear me not so swiftly o'er ;
Cease thy roaring, foamy ocean,
    I will tempt thy rage no more.

Ah ! within my bosom beating,
    Varying passions wildly reign ;
Love, with proud Resentment meeting,
    Throbs by turns, of joy and pain.

Joy, that far from foes I wander,
    Where their taunts can reach no more ;
Pain, that woman's heart grows fonder
    When her dream of bliss is o'er !

N

Love, by fickle fancy banish'd,
   Spurn'd by hope, indignant flies ;
Yet, when love and hope are vanish'd,
   Restless mem'ry never dies.

Far I go, where fate shall lead me,
   Far across the troubled deep ;
Where no stranger's ear shall heed me,
   Where no eye for me shall weep.

Proud has been my fatal passion !
   Proud my injured heart shall be !
While each thought, each inclination,
   Still shall prove me worthy *thee !*

Not one sigh shall tell my story ;
   Not one tear my cheek shall stain ;
Silent grief shall be my glory,—
   Grief, that stoops not to complain !

Let the bosom prone to ranging,
   Still by ranging seek a cure ;
Mine disdains the thought of changing,
   Proudly destin'd to endure.

Yet, ere far from all I treasur'd,
   * * * * * * * ere I bid adieu ;
Ere my days of pain are measur'd,
   Take the song that's still thy due !

Yet, believe no servile passions
   Seek to charm thy vagrant mind ;
Well I know thy inclinations,
   Wav'ring as the passing wind.

I have lov'd thee,—dearly lov'd thee,
   Through an age of worldly woe ;
How ungrateful I have prov'd thee
   Let my mournful exile show !

Ten long years of anxious sorrow,
   Hour by hour I counted o'er ;
Looking forward, till to-morrow,
   Every day I lov'd thee more !

MARY ANNE (" PERDITA ") ROBINSON
After a portrait by Romney

Pow'r and splendour could not charm me ;
　I no joy in wealth could see !
Nor could threats or fears alarm me,
　Save the fear of losing thee !

When the storms of fortune press'd thee,
　I have wept to see thee weep !
When relentless cares distress'd thee,
　I have lull'd those cares to sleep !

When with *thee*, what ills could harm me ?
　Thou couldst every pang assuage ;
But when absent, nought could charm me ;
　Every moment seem'd an age.

Fare thee well, ungrateful rover !
　Welcome Gallia's hostile shore ;
Now the breezes waft me over ;
　Now we part—TO MEET NO MORE.

On her return, Mary Anne contracted an intimacy
with Colonel (afterwards Sir Banastre) Tarleton, an
officer in the British Army in America. His affairs
were in disorder, and in taking a journey in connection with these she had an illness which deprived her
of the use of her limbs. "Thus, at four-and-twenty
years of age, in the pride of youth and the bloom of
beauty, was this lovely and unfortunate woman
reduced to a state of more than infantile helplessness,"
her daughter has written. "Yet, even under so severe
a calamity, the powers of her mind, and the elasticity
of her spirits, triumphed over the weakness of her
frame. This check to the pleasures and vivacity of
youth, by depriving her of external resource, led her
to the more assiduous cultivation and development
of her talents. But the resignation with which she
had submitted to one of the severest of human

calamities, gave place to hope, on the assurance of her physicians that by the mild air of a more southern climate she might probably be restored to health and activity." Mary Anne beguiled the tedium of her long confinement by the use of her pen. She wrote many poems, and some plays and tales, and also works of other kinds. These, however, added little to her income. "My mental labours have failed through the dishonest conduct of my publishers," she declared. "My works have sold handsomely, but the profits have been theirs." On March 29, 1800, she wrote : " I feel my health decaying, my spirit broken. I look back without regret that so many of my days are numbered, and, were it in my power to choose, I would not wish to measure them again." The end came on the following December 28. At her own request she was buried in the churchyard of Old Windsor.

A PASTORAL ELEGY
ON
The Death of Mrs. Robinson
By Peter Pindar

Farewell to the nymph of my heart !
Farewell to the cottage and vine !
From *these* with a tear, I depart,
Where pleasure so oft was *mine*.

Remembrance shall dwell on her smile,
And dwell on her lute and her song ;
That sweetly my hours to beguile,
Oft echoed the valleys along.

Once more the fair scene let me view,
The grotto, the brook, and the grove.
Dear valleys, for ever adieu !
Adieu to the DAUGHTER of LOVE !

DOROTHY JORDAN
(*née* BLAND)
1761–1816

DOROTHY JORDAN (*née* BLAND)
1761–1816

I

"THE Great Illegitimates : Public and Private Life of that Celebrated Actress, Miss Bland, otherwise Mrs. Ford, or Mrs. Jordan, late Mistress of H.R.H. the D. of Clarence, now William IV., Founder of the FitzClarence Family : delineating the Vicissitudes attendant on her Early Life ; the Splendour of her Noon-tide Blaze, as Mistress of the Royal Duke ; and her Untimely Dissolution at St. Cloud, near Paris—resulting from a Broken Heart. Accompanied by Numerous Remarks and Anecdotes of Illustrious and Fashionable Characters. By a Confidential Friend of the Departed."

The above is the title of a book published by J. Duncombe, 19 Little Queen Street, Holborn, in 1830, and it is now very rare ; indeed, there is no copy in the Library of the British Museum. It was, however, reprinted in 1886, with some excisions. The admirers of Mrs. Jordan had no cause to be grateful to her " Confidential Friend," for his work is a rather scandalous production. At the same time it is not to be denied that this " Public and Private Life " contains valuable biographical information.

Mrs. Jordan's mother, Grace Phillips, is said to have

been one of three daughters of " a Welsh dignitary
of the Church, possessed of a good living ; independent of which, his circumstances were affluent, and
his character as a divine, in every respect moral and
unimpeachable." In these circumstances it is surprising to read that all the girls went on the stage.
The earlier biographies have it that Grace Phillips
eloped at the age of sixteen with one Captain Bland, a
man of good family and of considerable fortune, and
was married in 1761 by the rites of the Roman Catholic
Church. Dorothea, or Dorothy, was born in the
following year at Waterford, Ireland. The story goes
that Bland's family resented the marriage and cut
off supplies ; that thereupon the young husband and
wife went on the stage, and that ultimately the
captain's father successfully instituted legal proceedings to an annulment of the marriage on the grounds
of nonage, " when the unfortunate wife was left with
a numerous progeny to struggle against every difficulty." " At the period to which we allude," we are
told, " Captain Bland had attained the rank of
Colonel ; when finding himself freed from the matri-
monial bond—unmindful of the duties of a father,
and the line of conduct honour should have pre-
scribed—he wholly abandoned his former partner, and
in a short time led to the hymeneal altar another
lady, possessed of an ample revenue ; allowing his
former wife a very mediocre stipend for the maintenance of herself and the numerous progeny she had
borne him." It is comforting to learn that retribution
followed. " Fortune, however, cannot control happi-

DOROTHY JORDAN
After a portrait by Rufsell

ness, and the wealth obtained by Colonel Bland proved no panacea to the stings of a goaded conscience : his former serenity soon vanished, and he died after a short lapse of time the victim of his own heartless conduct." Which goes to show that it is not only the good who die young. To conclude : " As the fortune of the second Mrs. Bland had been settled upon herself prior to marriage, in the event of the Colonel's death, his children by the former union were left totally destitute ; until actuated by sentiments of common humanity "—somewhat belatedly stirred, it might appear to those inclined to cavil—" his relatives afforded some relief to the offspring, but totally abandoned the mother to her cruel fate."

A truly heartrending tale, calculated to draw tears from all but the most callous. Actually, however, it bristles with improbabilities. Only one point shall be put forward : if Captain Bland left the Army to go on the stage, how did he rise to the rank of Colonel ?

It is probably true that Dorothy's mother was an actress at Smock Alley Theatre ; and, according to Joseph Knight, there is some reason to believe that her father, Bland, was merely a stage underling.

Anyhow, Dorothy, in 1777, was for some months assistant to a milliner in Dame Street, Dublin ; and later in that year, under the style of Miss Francis, appeared at Crow Street Theatre as Phœbe in *As You Like It*. Here, or at the theatre at Cork—where her father is said to have been a scene-shifter—she played Lopez, a male character, in *The Governess*, Priscilla

Tomboy in *The Romp*, and Adelaide in Jephson's
Count of Narbonne.

In 1781 Richard Daly acquired the lease of the
Smock Alley Theatre. He was a villain of the deepest
dye, of " she must and shall be mine," " once aboard
the lugger," kind. It was his practice to lend money
to the young actresses in his company, and then
threaten to have them imprisoned for debt unless they
yielded themselves to him. " The manner and person
of our heroine having attracted Mr. Daly's attention,"
the " Confidential Friend " relates, " he followed the
glorious precedent of many individuals holding similar
managerial stations : conceiving himself entitled to
command the favours of every lady in his service,
under pain of displeasure. Poor Miss Francis proved
too virtuous to submit, and for a period the unprincipled desires of her employer received a salutary
check from the stern dictates of innate virtue. Finding himself foiled, the unprincipled manager caused
his victim to be seduced to the residence of a dependent, where she was forcibly detained, and every
unfair advantage taken of her helpless condition."
An infamous fellow, Richard Daly !

Whether this is, or is not, the correct version of
the seduction, there is no doubt that Mrs. Jordan was
for a while, however brief, the mistress of Daly, by
whom she became with child. She certainly was
afraid of him, for she fled secretly, with her mother,
brother, and sister, to Leeds, where the family arrived
almost destitute. Leeds had probably been chosen
because Tate Wilkinson was manager of the theatrical

circuit, and Mrs. Bland had some acquaintance with him, having at Dublin in 1758 played Desdemona to his Othello. Wilkinson was willing to help so far as he could. He asked Dorothy what she could play : tragedy, comedy, farce ? to which she replied laconically, " All." When telling this story she always said, at this point of it : " In my life, I never saw an elderly gentleman more astonished ! "

Wilkinson consented to give this girl of twenty her chance, and on July 11, 1782, she, still under the name of Francis, appeared as Calista in Rowe's *The Fair Penitent.* It was not an evening of unalloyed pleasure for the manager, for he had yielded to Mrs. Bland's request that he would announce that, after the play, the young actress would sing the song of " The Greenwood Laddie." " Mrs. Jordan was heard throughout the play with the greatest attention and sympathy," James Boaden writes, " and the manager began to tremble at the absurdity, as he reasonably thought it, of Calista arising from the dead, and rushing before an audience in their tears, to sing a ballad in the pastoral style, which nobody called for or cared about. But on she jumped, with her elastic spring, and a smile that nature's own cunning hand had moulded, in a frock and a little mob cap, and her curls, as she wore them all her life ; and she sang her ballad so enchantingly as to fascinate her hearers and convince the manager that every charm had not been exhausted by past times, nor all of them numbered ; for the volunteer unaccompanied ballad of Mrs. Jordan was peculiar to her, and charmed only by *her* voice and manner. Leeds, though a manufacturing town, and strongly addicted to the interests of trade, was, at the call of the charmer, induced to crowd her benefit in August."

Wilkinson was pleased enough to give her an engagement at fifteen shillings a week—his high-water mark was a guinea. "Owing to the matronly condition in which she found herself," as it has been delicately put, "she soon changed her name to Mrs. Jordan. During the next few years she played at Leeds, or in other towns of the circuit, a considerable number of parts, so various, as Arionelle, Lady Teazle, Jane Shore, Lady Racket, Indiana, and Zara.

Mrs. Jordan was unquestionably a trial to her manager, but his good humour was proof against the pricks. When Richard Yates saw her as Fatima in the farce *Cymon,* he pronounced the actress "a mere piece of theatrical mediocrity"; but it is as likely as not that he was misled by seeing her on one of the days when she would not be troubled to act. Again, she was unreliable. She was announced to appear on March 5, 1785, for the benefit of Mrs. Mills, as singing an air at the termination of the third act of *Cymbeline* and performing in the afterpiece of *The Poor Soldier ;* but at the last moment she pleaded indisposition, and no persuasions could induce her to sing the song in question. No one believed in her excuse—she had cried "wolf" too often. She had, indeed—anyhow, at this time—the defects of her qualities.

These years on circuit—Leeds, Wakefield, Doncaster, and Sheffield—were of the greatest possible value to Mrs. Jordan, for it was during this period that she learnt the business. Not only Tate Wilkinson trained her " I introduced her," he writes, " to our critic, Mr. Cornelius Swan, of York, who said he would *teach her to act.* And when she was ill he was admitted to the little bed-chamber, where, by the side of the bed, with Mrs. Bland's old red cloak round his neck, he would sit and instruct his pupil in Hill's character of Zara. ' You must revive that tragedy, Wilkinson,' said he, ' for I have given the Jordan but three lessons, and she is so adroit at receiving my instructions, that I declare she repeats the character as well as Mrs. Cibber ever did ; nay, let me do the Jordan justice, for I do not exceed when with truth I declare, Jordan speaks it as well as I could *myself.*' " There was no false modesty about old Cornelius : on a report, in the decline of his life, that Garrick was about to resume the part of Othello, he sent him a long discourse intimating the way in which that character should be played. Cornelius adopted her, more or less, as his daughter ; but at his death did not leave her a penny.

On special occasions London " stars " adventured to northern towns. William (" Gentleman ") Smith, who had seen Mrs. Jordan during a race week at York, admired her so much that his description of her appearance and her ability fired the managers of Drury Lane Theatre to offer her an engagement at four pounds a week—with Tate Wilkinson she was only receiving thirty shillings—to play " second " to Mrs. Siddons. Mrs. Siddons, who had also seen her act, had no high opinion of her gifts, and remarked that, "She had better remain at York than venture on the London boards." The offer to go to Drury Lane was accepted, and Mrs. Jordan took her leave of the northern circuit at Wakefield on September 9, 1785, in *The Poor Soldier*.

In one act, at least, of her life, Mrs. Jordan showed wisdom. Mrs. Siddons was at the height of her fame, and the new-comer, realising the other's pre-eminence in tragedy, insisted on being permitted to make her London début in comedy, and appeared on October 18, 1785, as Peggy in Garrick's version of Wycherley's *The Country Girl*. Although it is certain that she did her utmost, it is more than probable that she was nervous : anyhow, she did not on this occasion rouse the audience or the critics to any considerable degree of enthusiasm—and this, in spite of the fact that Peggy was one of her favourite and most successful rôles. " Peggy," we have been told, " was unquestionably the *chef d'œuvre* of Mrs. Jordan's comic powers, and we despair of ever again witnessing the sterling *naïveté* with which she sustained that arduous personification throughout ; every scene possessed its characteristic excellencies ; but in that where she pens the letter in presence of, and after the exit of, her guardian, the powers of comic delineation had attained the highest pitch of excellence ; in short, the mimic art could extend the witchery of its influence no further." It was mainly her playing of Peggy that induced the management to raise her salary to twelve pounds a week, and to give her two Benefits.

Also, she received tribute from members of the public in the form of valuable presents ; while the club at Brooks's sent her a purse containing three hundred guineas. Thus were successful actresses honoured in her day !

During her first season at Drury Lane Mrs. Jordan, also played such different parts as Viola in *Twelfth Night*, Imogen, Miss Hoyden in *A Trip to Scarborough*, Hypolita in *She Would and She Would Not*, Mrs. Brady in *The Irish Widow*, Miss Lucy in *The Virgin Unmasked*, and created Rosa in James Cobb's comic opera *Strangers at Home*. At the end of the season she had established herself as a leading actress, and she remained at Drury Lane until 1809.

Mrs. Jordan, during the vacation in 1786, revisited Leeds, where she was received with acclamation. Tate Wilkinson asked her to play there one night, and she consented to do so, stipulating that they were to share the receipts after deducting fifteen pounds. The manager demurred, but finding the actress adamant, he consented with reluctance ; but *The Country Girl* and *The Romp* crowded the theatre, and the profit to each was ample. From Leeds Mrs. Jordan went to Edinburgh and thence to Glasgow, and scored successes in each city. So profitable were these provincial trips that she generally repeated them each summer.

At Drury Lane for years to come she was often cast for sentimental and even tragic parts, such as Helena in *All's Well that Ends Well*, Ophelia, Juliet, Rosalind, Beatrice, and the like, in which she was

probably no more than adequate. It was in comedy
that she made her great reputation, with Sir Harry
Wildair (as which Peg Woffington had scored so
heavily), Little Pickle in *The Spoiled Child*, Miss
Prue, Lady Teazle, Miss Hardcastle, and Lydia
Languish ; but it took the managers of the theatre
a long time to discover what the audiences had realised
at once, and even then she was given Angela in
" Monk " Lewis's *Castle Spectre* in 1797, Flavia in
Vortigerm and Cora in *Pizarro* two years later, and
Imogen in Lewis's *Adelmorn the Outlaw* in 1801. When
Elizabeth Farren retired from the stage in 1797, she
had the reversion of the parts usually played by that
actress, although, it has been said, " some of those
characters were outside her range."

Elizabeth Farren appeared for the last time on the
stage on April 8, 1797, when she played Lady Teazle,
on which occasion she delivered a farewell address to
a crowded home. She retired at the age of thirty-
eight to marry Edward, twelfth Earl of Derby, who
had been devoted to her for years. His wife had died
on March 14, and he married Miss Farren on May 1.

In the meantime another actress had arisen. This
was Harriot Mellow, who, after a training in the
provinces, had made her début at Drury Lane as
Lydia Languish. Her acting was not good, but her
beauty and her musical voice saved her from failure.
Experience gave her confidence, and she became
definitely one of the stock company at Drury Lane,
once playing Mrs. Jordan's part of Mrs. Amanthis in
The Child of Nature. She withdrew from the stage,

HARRIOT MELLON

After the engraving by Cooke

at the height of her fame, in 1815, to marry the octagenarian millionaire banker, Thomas Coutts, who dying seven years later, left her his entire fortune. In 1827 she married William Aubrey de Vere, ninth Duke of St. Albans. Though a stage rival of Mrs. Jordan, she was almost always eclipsed by her.

" Mrs. Jordan, four years ago only, playing at York at thirty-one shillings and sixpence a week, was thought really very clever by London performers who saw her there," so runs a passage in an early biography of Mrs. Abington, " but all said it would not do among them, yet by great luck, great good fortune indeed, and to be for an hundred years at least remembered in theatrical annals, she in two years afterwards made even the London managers dread her frown, her non-compliance, her elopement, her toothache, or her phantom of horror with which she has threatened them, to the terror of tragedy itself, and made them comply with the most exorbitant terms. A happy lot indeed ! A happy rise ! Mrs. Jordan is certainly the lucky child of fortune, but led, caressed, and nursed in the lap of Nature. She is undoubtedly the reigning Thalia of the age 1790, and deservedly so ; and to her comic talents, archness, whim, and fancy I submissively bow, and also acknowledge her humanity and goodness to her late parent, but am compelled as Mr. Manager, to declare, like Mr. Foote, in his *Devil on Two Sticks* (as greatness knows itself), that Mrs. Jordan, at making a bargain, is too many for the cunningest devil of us all."

o

She won golden tributes from the critics, and the opinions of some of those who saw her act must be given.

" Those who have only seen Mrs. Jordan within the last ten or fifteen years," Charles Lamb wrote in his essay " On Some of the Old Actors," " can have no adequate notion of her performance of such parts as Ophelia, Helena in *All's Well that Ends Well*, and Viola in *Twelfth Night*. Her voice had latterly acquired a coarseness, which suited well enough with her Nells and Hoydens, but in those days it sank, with her steady, melting eye, into the heart. Her joyous parts —in which her memory now chiefly lives—in her youth were outdone by her plaintive ones. There is no giving an account how she delivered the disguised story of her love for Orsino. It was no set speech that she had foreseen, so as to weave it into an harmonious period, line following line, to make up the music—yet I have heard it so spoken, or rather *read*, not without its grace and beauty—but, when she had declared her sister's history to be a ' blank,' and that she ' never told her love,' there was a pause, as if the story had ended—and then the image of the ' worm in the bud ' came up as a new suggestion—and the heightened image of ' Patience ' still followed after that, as by some growing (and not mechanical) process, though springing up after thought, I would almost say, as they were watered by her tears. So, in those fine lines—

' Write loyal cantos of contemned love—
Hollow your name to the reverberate hills—'

there was no preparation made up in the foregoing

image for what was to follow. She used no rhetoric in her passion ; or it was Nature's own rhetoric, when it seemed altogether without rule or law."

" A lady of the name of Alsop, a daughter of Mrs. Jordan (by a former husband), has appeared at Covent Garden theatre, in the character of Rosalind," Hazlitt wrote in his *View of the English Stage*, under the date of October 22, 1815. " Not only the circumstances of her relationship to that excellent actress, but the accounts in the papers raised our curiosity and expectations very high. We were unwillingly disappointed. The truth is, Mrs. Alsop is a very nice little woman, who acts her part very sensibly and cleverly, and with a certain degree of arch humour, but no more like her mother ' than I to Hercules.' When we say this, we mean no disparagement to this lady's talents, who is a real acquisition to the stage in correct and chaste acting ; but simply to prevent comparisons, which can only end in disappointment. Mrs. Alsop would make a better Celia than Rosalind. Mrs. Jordan's excellencies were all natural to her ; it was not as an actress, but as herself, that she charmed everyone. Nature has formed her in most prodigal humour, and when Nature is in this humour to make a woman all that is delightful, she does it most effectually. Mrs. Jordan was the same in all her characters, and inimitable in all of them, because there was no one else like her. Her face, her tears, her manners, were irresistible. Her smile had the effect of sunshine, and her laugh did one good to

hear it. Her voice was eloquence itself : it seemed
as if her heart was always at her mouth. She was all
gaiety, openness, and good nature. She rioted in her
fine animal spirits, and gave more pleasure than any
other actress, because she had the greatest spirit of
enjoyment in herself. Her Nell—— but we will not
tantalise ourselves or our readers. Mrs. Alsop has
nothing luxurious about her, and Mrs. Jordan was
nothing else. Her voice is clear and articulate, but
not rich or flowing. In person, she is small ; and her
face is not prepossessing. Her delivery of the speeches
was correct and excellent, as far as it went, but without much richness or power—lively good sense is
what she really possesses. She also sung the Cuckoo
Song very pleasingly.''

"As an actress," Genest says, "she never had a
superior in her proper line. Mrs. Clive no doubt
played Nell as well as Mrs. Jordan : it was hardly
possible for her to have played the part better. In
' breeches parts,' no actress can be put into compe-
tition with her but Mrs. Woffington. Though she
was never handsome, she sported the best leg ever
seen on the stage.''

Sir Joshua Reynolds delighted in a being " who ran
upon the stage as a playground, and laughed from
sheer wildness of delight." John Bannister declared
that " no woman ever uttered comedy like her . . .
she was perfectly good-tempered, and possessed the
best of hearts." Mrs. Siddons said of her in 1786 :
" We have a great comic actress now, called Mrs.
Jordan. She has a vast deal of merit ; but, in my

mind, is not perfection "—but then Mrs. Jordan's
Rosalind was preferred to that of Mrs. Siddons's.

The anonymous author of the *Memoirs of the Green-
room* also burst into praise in a lyrical effusion, styled
" A Poetical Character " :

" To make us feel ev'n GARRICK's love no more,
    And be what he and PRITCHARD were before,—
    Like them, an equal share of praise to gain,
    In mirth's gay sallies or the tragic strain.
    This to perform, at last did JORDAN come,
    And rais'd their buried graces from the tomb,
    When *Viola*, to hopeless flames a prey,
    Pines with her smother'd love, and fades away.
    Each sentence moves us, more from lips like those,
    And ev'ry line with added beauty glows !
    When wandering wild, to seek what climes afford
    Some certain tidings of her captive lord—
    Matilda roams ;—the melancholy strain,
    Wakes in each breast a gentle, pleasing pain :
    At that sad voice, the nerves responsive beat :
    ' It lends a very echo to the seat
    Where love is thron'd '—so soft it sounds that hence,
    The tuneful nothings steal the charms of sense.
    Again behold the *Country Girl* appears
    With arch simplicity. The Queen of Tears
    Flies far away : Mirth rules the sportive night,
    And all is rapture, laughter and delight !
    'Tis not the actress speaks—'tis Nature all :
    No tinsel tricks the wandering sense recall.
    Th' illusion lasts throughout—in ev'ry tone
    Unfetter'd genius stamps her for its own.
    Who that had only seen her in some part,
    Where, as in *Viola*, she charms the heart :
    Where ev'ry step is elegance ; and grace
    Informs each feature of that lovely face.
    Who that had seen her thus could e'er presume
    To think those sparkling eyes could still assume

The rolling vacancy and senseless stare
That marks the gawkiness of *Hoyden's* air ?
Or who that only had Matilda seen,
And the soft tenderness of *Richard's Queen*,
Would e'er conceive that the same form might show
The rakish freedom of a rattling beau !
Such are thy pow'rs, so vast and unconfin'd,
Quick as a thought, and shifting as the wind !
May wealth and fortune all thy steps attend,
And private worth retain the private friend ;
For, if report speaks true, that face imparts
An honest copy from the best of hearts—
The gen'rous feeling of a lib'ral mind,
And solid sense with gay good humour join'd."

II

It has been well said that Mrs. Jordan's domestic life was brilliant rather than happy. It may be added that it was so varied as to cause scandal in an age that was certainly not too straitlaced.

Her seduction by Richard Daly has been mentioned. It really would seem that his passion for her endured, even after it had been satisfied, for, when she was first in England, he tried to lure her back to him, it is true by threats to proceed against her, firstly, for debt, and, secondly, for having forfeited her articles at the Smock Alley Theatre. Cornelius Swan, who has earlier been mentioned, hearing that she was threatened with arrest, came to the rescue by paying all that was demanded—to the fury of the manager, who wanted the girl and not the money. So far as she was concerned, there was an end of Daly.

The daughter of this connection, Frances, married in 1809 one Alsop, a clerk in the Ordnance Office. Mrs. Jordan gave her a dowry of £10,000 and set up the young couple in a house in Golden Square, Soho. The marriage, unfortunately, was not a success, and it would seem that a separation was agreed upon. In 1815, as has been said, Mrs. Alsop went on the stage for a while—Hazlitt's opinion of her has been given—but she did not long remain in the profession. She went to America, where she died prematurely. Alsop, as will be stated, presently was the source of a great deal of trouble to his mother-in-law.

After she was established as a favourite at Drury Lane, she formed a connection with Richard Ford, a descendant of an old Sussex family, who in 1789 represented East Grinstead in the House of Commons. He was for some time an Under-Secretary of State, and subsequently was appointed chief police magistrate of London, and knighted. " It appears most probable that the pre-eminent talents of the lady, in the first instance, wrought upon the affections of Mr. Ford, who, being intimate with most of the first-rate performers, easily obtained an introduction to the acquaintance of Mrs. Jordan, soon after which he made a formal declaration of his passion ; this we know was accompanied by *a solemn promise of marriage*, which the gentleman said must be deferred, under the dread of giving offence to his father, on whom he was dependent ; when, confiding in the honour and promises of her suitor, Mrs. Jordan at length consented to place herself under his protection." Thus the actress's earliest biographer; and it can only be assumed that the biographer was more naïve than the lady, whose very considerable experience of life must have given her a very shrewd idea of the value of a promise of marriage at some unspecified date. "With Mr. Ford, she cohabited for many years *as his wife*, in full expectation that Sir Richard would become reconciled to the union at no very distant period; and the fruits of that connection were several children, who derived their entire support from the exertion of the mother, her fidelity to the gentleman she regarded as her husband having never been called into question, as the uniform conduct she pursued was so exemplary as to render her even a pattern of matronly excellence for every married woman. So invariably correct, indeed, was the conduct of the lady, that no suspicion was ever entertained respecting her not being legally the wife of Mr. Ford. Many instances illustrative of this fact might be adduced, but as one will speak for the rest, we beg to instance the names of Sir Francis Lunn, Bart., and his Lady, who resided in Argyle Street. They were in the habit of giving splendid routs, at which Mrs. Ford was constantly received as the wife of that gentleman, who uniformly attended such parties with his protégée; being by him introduced in the character of a married woman."

Mrs. Jordan had four children by Ford. One of the girls, Dora, married, in 1810, Frederick Edward March, a natural son of Lord Henry Fitzgerald, and, like Alsop, a clerk in the Ordnance Office; another,

HARRIOT MELLON
After the engraving by P. Roberts

Lucy, became the wife of Colonel (afterwards General) Hawker of the 14th Light Dragoons. " I am sure," Mrs. Jordan wrote to a friend, " you will be pleased to hear that your young friend, Lucy, is about to be married, to Colonel Hawker. He is a most excellent man, and has a very good private property. She will make the best of wives—a better girl never lived. It makes me quite happy, and I intend to give her to the value of £10,000."

The following letter, written in August, 1791, is interesting, not merely because it shows the writer's independence—she had not been pleased with the reception accorded her at her last appearance in the city—but also, and particularly, because of the signature :

" Sir,

" I agree with pleasure to your proposal of giving you thirty pounds rather than ever perform in York. I shall return to-morrow, and settle the balance of the account.

" I am, sir,

" Your obliged, humble servant,

" D. Ford."

Horace Walpole, writing on September 16, 1791, to the Misses Berry, says : " Do you know that Mrs. Jordan is acknowledged to be Mrs. Ford ? " On October 16, addressing the same correspondents, he writes : " Mrs. Jordan, whom Mr. Ford had declared his wife, and presented as such to some ladies at Richmond, has resumed her former name, and is said

to be much at a *principal* villa at Petersham, which
I do not affirm—far be it from me to vouch for a
quarter of what I hear. If I let my memory listen, it
is that I may have some ingredients for my letters,
and to which you are apprised not to give too much
credit, though, while absent [on the Continent], it is
natural to like to hear the breath of the day, which
at home you despise, as it commonly deserves."

About 1790, the Duke of Clarence began to look
upon Mrs. Jordan with eyes of favour. The mis-
guided Lady Lunn was much troubled, and observed
to a friend, "I shall again this evening instil into
Mrs. Jordan's mind the absolute necessity of *sticking*
to Mr. Ford, for I am well convinced that no good
will accrue from the princely association." "For a
time matters continued," we are told; "the royal
lover's importunities increasing, while pecuniary offers
were tendered in the way of settlement to the amount
of one thousand pounds *per annum*, which ultimately
led our heroine to conceive that it became a bounden
duty, on behalf of her offspring, to reflect seriously on
the subject. The ultimatum of this painful scrutiny
was a proposal on the part of Mrs. Jordan, that as
she had for so many years cohabited with Mr. Ford,
and borne him a family of children; in consideration
also of her having been uniformly introduced into
society as his wife, she conceived herself justly entitled
to his hand; and in consequence stipulated that Mr.
Ford should at once name a day to ratify the promise
so incessantly made, or, in the event of a refusal, she
conceived herself at liberty to act as the dictates of

prudence should prescribe. Mr. Ford, however, thought fit to evade the question, when our heroine conceived herself at liberty to embrace the protection offered by the Duke of Clarence ; as in that case, she conceived ample means would be placed at her disposal to provide for her offspring, in whose behalf no legal plea on Mr. Ford could be set forth."

It is extremely doubtful whether Ford would, in any circumstances, have married his mistress ; but malicious tongues gave it forth that, lest he should at the last moment weaken, it had been intimated that if he abandoned the lady, he would, when convenient, be given the post of a stipendiary magistrate. Of this, however, it is only fair to say, there is no proof forthcoming : on the other hand, in the nature of things, there could not be. Such arrangements are not usually set forth in writing. It is more charitable to think that the lovers were weary of each other.

Ford, with almost unparalleled impertinence, had the audacity to write the following testimonial for publication in the Press :

Richard Ford to Dorothy Jordan.

"*October* 14, 1791.

" Lest any insinuations should be circulated to the prejudice of Mrs. Jordan, in respect of her having behaved improperly towards her children, in regard to pecuniary matters, I hereby declare that her conduct has, in that particular, been as laudable, generous, and as like a fond mother, as in her present situation it was possible to be. She had, indeed, given up for their use every sixpence she has been able to save from her theatrical profits. She has also engaged herself to allow them £550 *per annum ;* and, at the same time, settled £50 a year upon her sister. It is but bare justice to her for me to assert this, as the father of those children.

"In gratitude for the care Mrs. Jordan has ever bestowed upon my children, it is my consent and wish that she shall, whenever she pleases, see and be with them, provided her visits are not attended by any circumstances which may be improper to them, or unpleasant to me."

Some contemporary writers have said that the public was disgusted with Mrs. Jordan, because of her licentiousness—if this is the case, she must indeed have been very casual and frequent in her amours, since not much in the way of private morality was expected from the actress of that day. Others have it that theatre-goers were irritated by the several absences from the stage occasioned by her being *enceinte.* What is certain is that there was a feeling against her sufficiently strong to make her consider it desirable to publish an explanation.

Dorothy Jordan to the Editor of the " Morning Herald."

" GOWER STREET [LONDON], *February* 4, 1788.

" MR. EDITOR,

"A variety of paragraphs having lately appeared in the newspapers, tending to convey an

insinuation that I have declined performing again at
Drury Lane Theatre, until I am announced in a
manner different from what I have been; I beg the
favour of you to insert this letter, as a positive denial
of such charge, and of the supposed circumstances on
which it is founded. A long continuance of severe
illness has alone been the cause of my absenting myself
from my duty to the proprietors and the public.

" I am, sir, etc.,

" DOROTHEA JORDAN."

Later, she again, through the medium of the Press,
appealed to the public :

" TREASURY OFFICE, DRURY LANE,

" *November* 30, 1791.

" I have submitted in silence to the unprovoked
and unmanly abuse which, for some time past, has
been directed against me, because it has related to
subjects about which the public could not be interested; but to an attack upon my conduct in my
profession, and the charge of want of respect and
gratitude to the public, I think it my duty to reply.

" Nothing can be more cruel and unfounded than
the insinuation that I absented myself from the
theatre, on Saturday last, from any other cause than
real inability, from illness, to sustain my part in the
entertainment.

" I have ever been ready and proud to exert myself
to the utmost of my strength, to fulfil my engagements

with the theatre, and to manifest my respect for the audience; and no person can be more grateful for the indulgence and applause with which I have been constantly honoured. I would not obtrude upon the public attention to anything which does not relate to my profession, in which *alone*, I may, without presumption, say, I am accountable to them; but thus called on, in the present instance, there can be no impropriety in my answering those who have so ungenerously attacked me—that if they could drive me from that profession, they would take from me the *only income* I have, or mean to possess, the whole earnings of which, upon the past, and one half for the future, I have settled upon my *children*. Unjustly and cruelly traduced as I have been upon this subject, I trust that this short declaration will not be deemed impertinent; and, for the rest, I appeal with confidence to the justice and generosity of the public."

Mrs. Jordan, on the following December 10, after performing the part of Roxalana in *The Sultan*, decided to address the audience:

" I should conceive myself utterly unworthy of your favour if the slightest mark of public disapprobation did not affect me very sensibly. Since I have had the honour and the happiness to strive here to please you, it has been my constant endeavour by unremitting assiduity, to merit your approbation. I beg leave to assure you, upon my honour, that I have never absented myself one minute from the duties of my profession, but from real indisposition. Thus, having invariably acted, I do consider myself under the public protection."

Mrs. Jordan, then, threw in her lot with the Duke of Clarence, and remained with him for nearly a score of years, during which period—her fecundity was remarkable—she bore him ten children, all of whom were given the surnames of Fitzclarence. Of course, the connection could not have been kept secret, even if there had been any desire or intention to do so.

Mrs. Jordan, of course, had somewhat to alter the style of her living: she took a larger house, she engaged more servants; she set up a carriage or two, and was frequently seen about town driving in her yellow chariot. Yet, she remained the same unassuming creature that she was when she first came to England, and the company at her entertainments were decidedly " mixed," in the sense that she did not refrain from inviting her earlier friends.

The Press, of course, made comment, and an earlier biographer was at pains to gather some of the paragraphs :—

" Mrs. Jordan has withstood the unbounded offers of a certain personage ; so much to her own credit, and to the satisfaction of a certain gentleman, to whom she has for some years *afforded* her smiles, that the latter has, from motives of gratitude and love, introduced her as his *wife*, and in that character she has been received in the most fashionable circles."

" *A favourite comic actress*, if old *Goody Rumour* is to be trusted, has thought proper to put herself under the protection of a *distinguished sailor*, who *dropped anchor* before her last summer, at Richmond. As she resolutely held out, however, at that time, though the assault was vigorously pushed, perhaps this is only a flying report; and the lady thinks there is more security in a private *ford*, than in the *open sea*."

" *Little Pickle's* assumed character of the *Tar*, was a prelude only to her future nautical fame; for, though pressed into the service, she has consented, we find, to be close moored under the guns of the *Royal Commodore*."

" A Correspondent observes, that what was only a FORD*able* some time ago, is now capable of bearing a *first rate*."

" The part of *Mrs. Ford* has been supported with so much decorum at Richmond, by Mrs. Jordan, that many respectable familes there, are disposed to consider her as *quite the character*."

" A FACT. The *Naval Officer*, who too often infests the scenes of the Haymarket Theatre, to the annoyance of everyone that belongs to the house, *but one*, had the modesty the other day, to desire Mr. S—— to forbid Mr. Ford the privilege of appearing behind the scenes. Mr. S—— very properly told the *Naval Officer*, that Mr. Ford's *behaviour*, as a *gentleman*, precluded such a prohibition; and that, on point of *right*, Mr. Ford had as much pretension as (Mr. S——) himself." (December 13, 1791.)

" *Little Pickle's* carriage is to be immediately

decorated with something like *heraldic bearings :* a crest is already fixed upon, and what can be more appropriate than a *sea gull !*" (May 1, 1792.)

The Duke of York having been sent into the army, the Duke of Clarence entered the navy. At the age of thirteen he went to sea as a midshipman, and he very literally followed the injunction of his father to fight his way, by fighting a brother midshipman. He served under Keith, Hood, and Nelson—of the last, with an unwonted exercise of wit, he remarked that " his tail seems more than he has strength to carry." Nelson wrote to Captain Loch in complimentary terms of William, when he was in command of H.M.S. *Pegasus :* " In his professional life, he is superior to nearly two-thirds, I am sure, of the list, and in attention to orders and respect to his superior officer, I hardly know his equal. His Royal Highness keeps up strict discipline in his ship, and, without paying him any compliment, she is one of the finest ordered frigates I have seen."

The Duke of Clarence had no liking for Court life. Unlike his eldest brother, George, he had no hankering for magnificence. Carlton House would have bored him, and the Pavilion at Brighton would have had no allure for him. Ceremonial, so dear to this brother, Edward, Duke of Kent, irked him, and he avoided it whenever he possibly could. For some time he lived quietly and, therefore, happily, at Richmond, walking unattended about the streets, with an umbrella tucked under an arm ; but Horace Walpole in 1789 wrote : " The Duke of Clarence, no wonder, at his

P

age "—[he was then twenty-four]—" is already weary of a house in the middle of a village, with nothing but a green short apron to the river, a situation only fit for an old gentlewoman, who has to put out her knee-pads, and loves cards. He pays his bills regularly himself ; locks up his doors at night, that his servants may not stop out late ; and never drinks but a few glasses of wine. Though the value of crowns is mightily fallen of late at market, it looks as if his Royal Highness thought they were still worth waiting for. Nay, it is said, he tells his brothers he shall be King before either—this is fair, at least." William was not quite right. His brother George lived to ascend the throne in 1820, and to sit on it for ten years ; but the Duke of York obligingly died in 1827, and so made way for William.

When the Duke met Mrs. Jordan, he had been appointed Ranger of Bushy Park, and at Bushy House she lived, in the intervals of her theatrical engagements. The King was shocked at the *liaison*, and horrified when he heard of the allowance made to the actress.

" ' What, what !—you keep an actress ? ' said his Majesty to his son.

" ' Yes, sir,' he answered, readily enough.

" ' How much do you allow her ? What, what ? '

" ' A thousand a year.'

" ' A thousand a year ! ' said his Gracious Majesty, in astonishment. ' What, what ? That's too much. Give her five hundred. What, what, what ? ' "

It is recorded that when the Duke told his mistress of this conversation, she took a theatre programme, and, underlining certain words, handed it to him : the words were to the point, " *No money returned after the rising of the curtain.*"

As a matter of fact, there was no reason for his Majesty's indignation at his son's extravagance, for though there is not documentary evidence for it, it is as nearly certain as can be that Mrs. Jordan contributed to the expenses of their establishment—so considerably, indeed, that when the connection was broken off, though she had been earning a very large income—it has been estimated at £7000 a year —she was in poor circumstances. The public certainly were under the belief that she bore more than her share of the expenditure from the very beginning of the *liaison*, for the following paragraphs appeared in the Press on, respectively, November 3 and November 13, 1791 :

" The connection between *Little Pickle* and her new FRIEND has been paragraphed in every public shape, and, unless something extraordinary should occur, may now be dropped. We have only to add that, as *Banker to her Highness*, he actually received her *week's salary* from the *Treasurer*, on Saturday last."

" *On a Certain Person's receiving a Theatrical Salary.*

" As Jordan's high and mighty squire,
  Her play-house profits deign to skim ;
  Some folks audaciously enquire,
  If *he* keeps *her*, or *she* keeps *him* !
                                PINDAR JUNR.

" It is said positively to be a fact, that the actress, whose *elevated connection* has lately engrossed so much newspaper comment, has not *touched*, and is in little likelihood of obtaining, any pecuniary aid from her new protector ; and that, besides her domestic support, to which her own salary contributes, she has only procured an annuity for her eldest child, for which she is supposed to be indebted to an Irish manager of well-known gallantry [Richard Daly]."

Mrs. Jordan continued faithful to her profession, though, of course, her being so often with child made her appearances intermittent. Her popularity, however, was never greater—perhaps her association with the Duke of Clarence made people even more interested in her. As an instance of her vogue, William Holland, in 1789, published " Jordan's Elixir of Life, and Cure for the Spleen ; or, A Collection of all the Songs sung by Mrs. Jordan since her first appearance in London." This production, which contains forty-one songs, a brief biographical sketch, and an engraving of the actress in the part of Harry Wildair, found a ready sale: it is now very difficult to come by.

The following quaint composition appeared in the *Morning Herald* for October 20, 1790 :

" SEPULCHRAL ANTICIPATION.

" Near a monument to Mrs. Clive is a superb and richly decorated urn, entwined with a wreath of fading flowers, and embossed with a figure of Death trampling on the mask and emblems of Comedy. On the tomb is the subsequent inscription :—

SACRED TO THE MEMORY
of
MRS. DOROTHY JORDAN
Late of Drury Lane Theatre.

Poor injured mortality !
Snatched
From the fostering embrace of
Public admiration,
In the full vigour of her attraction
That raised it ;—
Stop, gazer,
And behold the little tyrant of hearts,
The favoured nymph of Euphrosyne ;
Thus mournfully entombed !
Disdaining
To wear the trammels of science, which too often
Prevent the intention, and restrain
The effect of the Drama ;
Her exertions were
The dictates of Nature,
Whose steps it was her profession to follow :
Like the Child of Fancy,
In wood notes wild,
She inspired the hearts of her hearers
With the warmth of sensibility,
And the transports of mirth :

The stern speculation of the pedantic critic (that too often blasts the *Genius of the Stage*, to maintain a consequence and authority, equally base and unwarrantable) :

Lost in the magic of her talents,
Would smooth its wrinkled front.
And, like honest Laughter,
Shake its bursting sides :
The jovial heart
That gave lustre to her scenic charms,
Cherished a sweetness of disposition,
Which rendered her amiable in private life ;

Her gaiety was decent,
As the heart that prompted it was sincere ;
And the frolic humour of the characters
It was her province to represent
As an ACTRESS,
She scorned to degrade the dignity
That belonged to her own, as a WOMAN.
In all her rosy train,
Thalia had not such a Nymph.
Tho' traveller, thou had'st not witnessed
The powers of which thou read'st,
Refuse not the tribute of a sigh
To her whose voice was
Public joy ;
Nor quit these hallowed mansions,
Till in the ardour of, a STERNE,
And the language of a SHAKESPEARE,
Thou hast exclaim'd,
' ALAS ! POOR JORDAN ! '

———

This monument is the tribute of
An impartial admirer
Unconnected with the theatre,
Whose only design was to join in that
Approbation of Mrs. Jordan,
Which the public so unanimously testified,
And which her exertions
So justly merited."

The season after Mrs. Jordan had accepted the protection of the Duke of Clarence she did not perform, and it was rumoured that it was her intention to retire from the stage, since his Royal Highness had made adequate provision for her : whereupon she wrote the following letter, which duly appeared in the Press :

Dorothy Jordan to R. B. Sheridan, Drury Lane Theatre.

" SOMERSET STREET [LONDON], *January* 29, 1793.

" SIR,

" From the very handsome manner in which you acceded to my proposals, and, as I conceived, concluded my engagement, I flattered myself I should have no difficulty to encounter in immediately entering into my agreement with you ; an event I have waited for with increased anxiety, from the circumstance of having, through your liberality, been for some time in the receipt of a very large salary, without being permitted to perform.

" I am totally at a loss to account for the conduct of the Manager [John Philip Kemble], in any other way than his *continued disinclination* to let me appear in any new character whatever—a complaint I have often been constrained to make to you, and you have as often acknowledged the justice of it ; and, in our last negotiation, endeavoured effectively to remove, but without success.

" As a duty I owe myself and the public, I mean to publish a copy of this letter, to serve as a simple, but *fair*, contradiction to some malicious reports that are circulated, insinuating that I have withdrawn myself from their protection, a circumstance I have every reason to be proud, and of which I shall ever retain the most grateful remembrance, accompanied by the sincerest regret at being deprived of the happiness of manifesting, in the duties of my profession, the truth of this *assertion*.

" You, sir, I make no doubt, will candidly confess, that I have already been too much tormented with regard to this engagement, and also that from this unnecessary delay in bringing forward the comedy, that it is now void ; and when I assure you that my situation in the theatre has, for a considerable time, been made very irksome to me, and that should I attempt to continue in it, *out of respect to you*, I should subject myself to still greater perplexities, which it is not in your power to prevent. I am, therefore, confident that you will release me from that kind of embarrassment, which the liberality of your conduct towards me, makes me suffer in the justice of my wish to quit the *Haymarket Theatre.*

" In complying with the above request, you will greatly add to the favours already conferred on,

" Sir,

" Yours, etc.,

" Dor. Jordan."

It must here be explained that during the rebuilding of Drury Lane, Mrs. Jordan was with the company at the King's Theatre in the Haymarket, where during 1792 she created the parts of the heroine of *The Village Coquette*, Julia Wingrove in *The Fugitive*, and Clara in *The French Duellist*. She soon, however, returned to Drury Lane.

" Nell of Clarence plays Ophelia to-night at Richmond," Horace Walpole wrote to Mary Berry on August 19, 1795 ; and a week later added : " My next paragraph the Darrels probably know, and may have told you : it was printed at the bottom of the playbills at Richmond last week, that Mrs. Jordan would not perform, as it was the birthday of his Royal Highness the Duke of Clarence—no, to be sure, she could not, for the Prince of Orange was to dine with him, and she did the honours at the head of the table—no, the Princesses were not there."

The fact that Mrs. Jordan acted as hostess at Bushy House seems to have irritated the Press more than her connection with the Duke, and the *Courier* in 1806 published the following ironical article :

" The Duke of Clarence's birthday was celebrated with much splendour in Bushy Park, on Thursday. The grand hall was entirely new fitted up with bronze pilasters, and various marble imitations ; the ceiling was correctly clouded, and the whole illuminated with some brilliant patent lamps, suspended from a beautiful eagle. The dining room, in the right wing, was fitted up in a modern style, with new elegant lamps at the different entrances. The pleasure-grounds was disposed for the occasion, and the servants had new liveries. In the morning, *the Duke of York's and Kent's bands arrived in caravans.* . . . The Duke of Kent's played some of the choruses and movements from Hadyn's oratorio of *The Creation, arranged by command of his Royal Highness*, for a band of wind instruments. About five o'clock, the Prince of Wales, the Dukes of York, Kent, Sussex, and Cambridge, Colonel Paget, etc., arrived from reviewing the Ger-

man Legion. After they had dressed for dinner, they
walked in the pleasure-grounds, accompanied by the
Lord Chancellor, Earl and Countess of Athlone and
daughter, Lord Leicester, Baron Hotham and Lady,
Baron Eden, the Attorney-General, Colonels Paget
and McMillan, Sergeant Marshall, and a number of
other persons.

"At seven o'clock, the second bell announced the
dinner, when the PRINCE took MRS. JORDAN *by the hand,
led her into the dining-room, and seated her at the top
of the table.* The Prince took his seat *at her right hand,*
and the Duke of York *at her left;* the Duke of Cambridge sat next to the Prince, the Duke of Kent next
to the Duke of York, and the Lord Chancellor next
to his Royal Highness. The DUKE OF CLARENCE *sat
at the foot of the table.* . . .

"The Duke of Clarence's NUMEROUS FAMILY *were
introduced,* and admired by the Prince, the Royal
Dukes, and the whole company; an infant in arms,
with a most beautiful white head of hair, was brought
into the dining-room by a nursery-maid. . . .

"The representing of the oratorio of *The Creation,*
and arranged by the Duke of Kent too, applied to the
purpose of ushering in the ' *numerous family* ' of the
Duke of Clarence—thus representing the Duke of
Kent as employed in an act, whereby the procreation
of a brood of illegitimate children is put in comparison
with the great works of the Almighty is, in the view
of this writer, an act of most indiscreet disloyalty, and
of blasphemy the most daring.

"We all know that the Duke of Clarence is not

married, and that, therefore, if he had children, those children must be bastards, and that the father must be guilty of a crime in the eye of the law, as well as of religion. . . . Can we hesitate in declaring that to represent the Duke of Clarence as having a ' numerous family of children,' is foully to slander his Royal Highness, and that further to represent him as *ostentatiously* exhibiting this ' numerous family ' in public, and in the immediate presence of all his Royal brothers, and of the Lord Chancellor of England and others of the nobles, is to accuse him of a gratuitous and wanton insult against the laws, manners, and morals of the country.

" This representation and accusation I must and do, therefore, consider as *false*, and I am confirmed in my opinion when I hear the same writer assert that the Prince of Wales took *Mother Jordan by the hand*, and, in the presence of a Countess, a Countess's daughter, and a Baroness, *seated her at the head of the table*, taking his place upon her right hand, his Royal brothers arranging themselves according to their rank, on both sides of the table, the *post of honour* being nearest Mother Jordan, who, the last time I saw her, cost me eighteen-pence in her character of Nell Jobson. This part of the account proves the falsehood of the whole ! . . .

" Being fully convinced of these important truths, I venture to beseech the royal parties whose names have been so unwarrantably brought before the public in the above cited publication, to cause a formal contradiction thereof to be publicly made. I venture to beseech them to reflect on the fatal consequences, which have uniformly ensued, and especially in recent instances, from proceedings such as are here described in this publication, and to remember that to be blameless as they doubtless are, is not enough, unless they are thought to be blameless."

III

James Boaden gives a picture of Mrs. Jordan at home in 1799. " It was about this piece " [*The Secret*, by Morris], " I remember, we had been speaking, when she told me she had another ' East Indian ' offered at her shrine, which she would trouble me to read. I did so, and we talked the piece over at her town residence in Somerset Street, Portman Square. She had not told me who was the author of the play. But there was that in it which merited consideration. I gave her my opinion frankly, and pointed out the indecorum of the interest. However, though not a moral play, it was written evidently, I said, by a man of talent ; and, as a benefit piece, preferable to an old one. Mrs. Jordan here, in confidence, informed me that the Duke had taken the trouble to read it, at her desire ; and that we agreed most decisively in our opinions. She was in charming spirits, I remember, that morning ; and occasionally ran over the strings of her guitar. Her young family were playing about us and the present Colonel George FitzClarence, then a child, amused me much, with his spirit and strength ; he attacked me, as his mother told me, his fine-tempered father was accustomed to permit him to do himself."

About 1809 the Press recorded rumours about the ménage at Bushey House, and it was suggested that there were quarrels between Mrs. Jordan and the Duke. The Press was, indeed, so violent that his Royal Highness begged his mistress to withdraw—temporarily, at any rate—from the stage.

The following letters were written by Mrs. Jordan to a confidential friend, whose name, however, has not transpired.

"BUSHY HOUSE, *Sunday*. [1809.]

"DEAR SIR,

"I should be very ungrateful indeed, if I could for a moment consider as an enemy, one from whom I have received very decided proofs of kindness and attention. I love candour and truth on all occasions, and the frankness with which you speak of my professional merits, stamps a value on your opinion of them, and which (*entre nous*) I really believe is quite as much as they deserve ; but we do not feel inclined to quarrel with the world for thinking better of us than we deserve.

"I do not know how to thank you for the humanity with which you seem to enter into my feelings ; they are, indeed, very *acute*, and did you know the three incomparable and truly amiable objects of my anxiety, you would not be inclined to withdraw your sympathy.

"With regard to the report of my quarrel with the Duke, every day of our past and present lives must

give the lie to it. He is an example for half the fathers
and husbands in the world, the best of masters, and
the most firm and generous of friends. I will, in a
day or two, avail myself of your kind offer to contradict these odious and truly wicked reports. I am
so ill that I can do nothing myself, but must wait for
the assistance of a good and clever friend, who is at
present out of the way, and who (if truth is not quite
scared out of the world) will endeavour to do away
with the ill impression those reports were meant to
make.

" In the meantime, accept my thanks, and believe
me,

" Yours truly,

" Dor. Jordan."

" Bushy House, March 27, 1809.

" Dear Sir,

" When I last did myself the pleasure of
writing to you, I mentioned that I waited for the
assistance of a friend who was not then just in the
way, to contradict the cruel and infamous reports that
were then in circulation ; but on my application to
him (perhaps he was right) he said that what had *been
done* had every good effect that could possibly be
expected or wished for ; and that a *renewal* of the
subject might do more harm than good.

" Of this, I should like to have *your opinion*, when
you have read the enclosed. I need not add that you
will set the author down for a very partial friend
indeed. In obedience to the Duke's wishes, I have

withdrawn myself for the present, or, at least, till there is a Theatre Royal for me to appear in.

" Mr. March and Mr. Alsop, the two gentlemen to whom my daughters are married, will do themselves the pleasure of leaving their cards at your door, next week.

" I ever am, sir,

" Your obliged, humble Servant,

" DOR. JORDAN."

" I am to play to-morrow week at the Opera House, and, as it is likely to be my *last night*, it would not be amiss to have it insinuated into the boxes."

" [1809.]

" DEAR SIR,

" Having frequently experienced your kindness in assisting me to do away with any unfair impression, your candour, believe me, cannot be better employed than in the defence of three as good and virtuous girls as ever existed.

" It would be painful to me, and unnecessary to you, to mention the cruel and infamous reports for some time in circulation, and to the extent of which I was really a stranger till last week. To say it has made me sick at heart, is saying little.

" I remain,

" Your obliged humble Servant,

" DOR. JORDAN."

"BATH, *Sunday, April* 22, 1809.

"DEAR SIR,

"I should be more insensible than my heart tells me I am, if I did not experience much gratification from your very kind and friendly letters—friendly, they must be, for though I am ever asking favour of you, I feel it impossible that I can ever return them.

"My professional success through life has indeed been most *extraordinary*, and consequently attended with *great emoluments*; but from my first starting in life, at the early age of fourteen, I have always had a large family to support. My mother was a duty; but on *brothers* and *sisters* I have lavished more money than can be supposed; and more, I am sorry to say, than I can well justify to those who have a stronger and prior claim on my exertions.

"With regard to myself (as much depends upon our ideas of riches), I have certainly enough; but this is too selfish a consideration to weigh one moment against what I consider to be a duty. I am quite tired of the profession. I have lost those great excitements, *vanity* and *emulation*; the first has been amply gratified, and the last I see no occasion for; but still, without these, it is a mere money-getting drudgery.

"The enthusiasm of the good people here is really ridiculous; but it brings 'grist to the mill,' and I shall, notwithstanding the great drawback of unsettled weather, clear between this place and Bristol, from £800 to £900.

" Though I very seldom go out when from home, I was tempted by my dear girl to go to a fashionable library, to read the papers, and, not being known, was entertained by some ladies with a most *pathetic* description of the parting between me and the Duke. My very dress was described, and the *whole conversation accurately repeated !* Unfortunately for the *party*, a lady came in who immediately addressed me by *name*, which threw them into the most ridiculous and (I conceive) embarrassing situation imaginable. In pity to them, I left the place immediately, and flatter myself I did not show any disgust or ill-nature on the occasion.

" The last favour I asked of you, was not to gratify my vanity, but my *best friends ;* who, in spite of the world, are, I can assure you, as much interested in me as they were seventeen years ago.

" Believe me ever, your truly obliged,

" DOR. JORDAN."

" DUBLIN, *Sunday, June* 18, 1809.

" DEAR SIR,

" I had left Bushy for this place, before the arrival of your letter. That you would enter into my feelings respecting my dear boy [George FitzClarence], I was convinced when I sent you the extract, and, as you very rightly supposed, only meant for your own perusal—for, however gratifying it might be to my feelings to see any testimonial of his good conduct before the world, I have reason to believe that *he* would be very angry with me if he thought I had

Q

made it public. I only mention this to show that he is an unassuming, modest boy ; so much so, that we could never get him to speak of the business at Corunna, where he was himself concerned ; but the accounts of him from every other quarter were indeed most gratifying.

"With regard to myself, I have not much to say : the audience are, of course, very kind, and my reception was most brilliant; but, *entre nous*, I do not think I shall make as much money as I expected.

"With every good wish, I remain, dear Sir,

"Your most obliged Servant,

"DOR. JORDAN."

Mrs. Jordan was not happy during her brief season at Dublin. The manager, Jones, was incompetent, and he had gathered together a more than indifferent company to support the "star." "A fellow of the name of Corri had raised himself to some notice by the continuance of his libels on Mrs. Jordan and her friends, among whom he was certainly warranted to include Sir Jonah Barrington and his family," James Boaden writes. "Sir Jonah [who was a Judge in the Irish Court of Admiralty] prosecuted the printer, and did everything that could be done to restrain the ungentlemanly and malapert exuberance of Mr. Gold, who was counsel for the defendant. His speeches, highly disgraceful to him, came into the public prints, and greatly annoyed Mrs. Jordan."

Dorothy Jordan to Sir Jonah Barrington.

" BUSHY HOUSE, *Wednesday* [*August,* 1809].

" MY DEAR SIR,

" Not having the least suspicion of the business in Dublin, it shocked and grieved me very much ; not only on my own account, but I regret I should have been the involuntary cause of anything painful to you, or to your amiable family. But of Mr. Jones I can believe anything, and I beg you will do me the justice to believe that my feelings are not selfish.

" Why, indeed, should I expect to escape their infamous calumnies ? Truth, however, will force its way, and justice exterminate that nest of vipers. I wanted nothing from Mr. Crompton's generosity ; but I had a claim on his justice—his honour.

" During the two representations of *The Inconstant,* I represented to him the state Mr. Dwyer was in, and implored him out of respect to the audience, if not in pity to my terrors, to change the play. As to the libel on Mr. Dwyer, charged to me by Mr. Gold, I never directly or indirectly, by words or by writing, demeaned myself by interfering in the most remote degree with so wretched a concern.

" I knew no editor—I read no newspapers while in Dublin. The charge is false and libellous on me—published, I presume, through Mr. Gold's assistance. Under that view of the case, he will feel himself rather unpleasantly circumstanced, should I call on him either to prove or disavow his assertions. To be introduced any way into such a business, shocks and grieves me; he might have pleaded for his companions without calumniating me—but, for the present, I shall drop an irksome subject, which has already given me more than ordinary uneasiness.

"Yours, etc.,

"Dor. Jordan."

Dorothy Jordan to a Friend.

"Bushy House, *Thursday, August* 17, 1809.

"Dear Sir,

"I am very vain, but still I have judgment enough not to be fond of doing that which I do very ill. Still, I feel pleasure in writing to you who so kindly enter into all my feelings. You may easily guess what they were last Monday night, when I heard the account of the battle of Talavera. Five thousand killed!—the Duke at Brighton—I went to bed, but not to sleep.

"The Duke set out at five o'clock on the Tuesday, to be the first to relieve me from my misery. I am mentally relieved; but it has torn my nerves to pieces. I have five boys, and must look forward to a life of constant anxiety and suspense. I am at present very ill—excuse this hasty scrawl, and believe me,

"Your ever obliged,

"Dora Jordan."

Though there had been no quarrel between Mrs. Jordan and her royal lover, a certain coldness, anyhow, on his part, had arisen, and the actress had removed in 1810 from Bushy House to a villa at Hammersmith. The separation, however, was not final until she had an interview with him one night at Maidenhead—after this, they never met again. It has been surmised that the determining cause of the separation was want of money. To Mrs. Jordan's credit, she would never allow that his Royal Highness had behaved dishonourably, and without consideration—what she thought is another matter.

The following letters are presumably to the friend with whom she had lately been in communication.

"BUSHY HOUSE, *Saturday* [1810].

"MY DEAR SIR,

"I received yours and its enclosure safe this morning.

"My mind is beginning to feel somewhat reconciled to the *shock* and *surprise* it has lately received; for could *you*, or the *world*, believe that we never had, for twenty years, the *semblance* of a quarrel. But this is so well known in our domestic circle, that the astonishment is the *greater!* MONEY, money, my good friend, or the *want* of it, has, I am convinced, made him at this moment the most wretched of men; but having done *wrong*, he does not like to retract. But with all his excellent qualities, his domestic virtues, his love for his lovely children, what must he not at the moment *suffer?* His distress should have been relieved *before*—but this is *entre nous*.

"All his letters are full of the most unqualified

praise of my conduct ; and it is the most heartfelt
blessing to know that to the best of my power, I have
endeavoured to deserve it.   I have received the
greatest kindness and attention from the Regent and
every branch of the Royal Family, who, in the *most
unreserved terms*, deplore this melancholy business.
The whole correspondence is before the Regent, and
I am proud to add that my *past and present conduct*
has secured me a friend, who *declares* he will never
forsake me.

" My forbearance, he says, is beyond what he could
have imagined—but what will not a woman do, who
is firmly and sincerely attached ?   Had he left me to
starve, I would never have uttered a word to his disadvantage.   I enclose you two other letters, and in a
day or two you shall *see more*, the rest being in the
hands of the Regent.

" And now, my dear friend, do not hear the Duke
of Clarence unfairly abused.   He has done *wrong*, and
he is *suffering* for it ; but as far as he has left it in
his *own power*, he is doing everything *kind* and *noble*,
even to the distressing *himself*.

" I thank you sincerely for the friendly caution at
the end of your letter, though I trust there will be no
occasion for it ; but it was kind and friendly, and as
such I shall ever esteem it.

" I remain, dear sir,

" Yours sincerely,

" DOR. JORDAN.

" Those letters are for your eye alone."

" My dear Sir,

"I should be sorry the letters I have enclosed to you were the only vouchers I could produce to the world, if necessary. But, good God! what will not the world say? I received two letters this day, telling me I was accused of *intrigueing* with the Duke of Cumberland!

"I am heart-sick, and almost worn out with this cruel business; but

"I am,

Yours very gratefully,

"Dor. Jordan."

"Bushy House, *Thursday* [1810].

"My dear Sir,

"Allow me to thank you for your kind attention to my request. We really live so much in the country, and so entirely within ourselves, that we might be dead and buried, without our friends knowing even that we had been ill. I have the heartfelt happiness of informing you, that the Duke is considerably better, though far from being as we could wish; however, his physicians have given his Royal Highness permission to go to town to-morrow. I have been confined ever since my return, owing to the fatigues and anxiety I have gone through. I hear it will be some time before I recover the very great *shock* I received. I hear there are to be two Drury Lanes; I believe just as likely as one.

"Yours ever,

"Dor. Jordan."

" CADOGAN PLACE [LONDON], *Thursday* [1810].

" MY DEAR SIR,

" I fear I must have appeared unmindful of your many kindnesses, in having been such a length of time without writing to you ; but really, till very lately, my spirits have been so depressed, that I am sure you will understand my feelings when I say, it costs me more pains to write to those interested about me, than to a common acquaintance. But the constant kindness and attention I meet with from the Duke, in every respect, but personal intercourse (and which depends as much on my feelings as his), has in a great measure restored me to my former health and spirits. Among many noble traits of goodness, he has lately added one more, that of exonerating me from my promise of not returning to my profession. This he has done, under the idea of its benefiting my health, and adding to my pleasures and comforts ; and though it is very uncertain, whether I shall ever avail myself of this kindness, yet you, if you choose, are at liberty to make it known, whether publicly or privately.

" Yours ever,

" DOR. JORDAN.

" I wish I could see you, but it is such a long way for you to come."

" [1811].

" MY DEAR SIR,

" I lose not a moment in letting you know that the Duke of Clarence has concluded and settled on me and his children, the most liberal and generous provisions ; and I trust everything will sink into oblivion.

"Yours ever,

"Dor. Jordan."

The terms were, for the maintenance of herself, her daughters, and her earlier family, an income of £4400 ; but in case of her returning to the stage the care of the Duke's daughters and the allowance for their maintenance were to revert to the Duke.

Since there was no quarrel between Mrs. Jordan and the Duke of Clarence, and a strong bond of affection still united them, it is necessary to look for the reason for their separation. It is not far to seek. Pressure was being brought to bear on the Duke of Clarence to marry, so as to secure the succession. George had only a daughter, Charlotte [who died in 1817 in child-birth], and as he was not living with his Consort, Caroline of Brunswick, there was no possibility of further legitimate issue. The Duke of York had no children. William, though he was happy enough as he was, was prepared to marry—on terms. His conditions were that his debts should be paid, and his children provided for. In 1811, being financially harassed, he proposed to the wealthy heiress, Miss Tylney Long.

> "And since no female can withstand
> The tempting offer of your hand,
> On fair Miss T——y L——g bestow
> Title, and equipage, and show."

The lady declined the honour, and hurriedly married William Pole Wellesley, fourth Earl of Mornington. His Royal Highness was not discouraged. He informed Lord Keith, that he desired to marry his daughter, Margaret ; but that young lady declined, and presently engaged herself to the Comte de Flahault. Again he was not discouraged. In the " Jerningham Letters," it is mentioned, under the date of February 27, 1818 : " It is said that the Duke of Clarence has proposed himself to Miss Wykeham, an heiress who has inherited from her grandmother all Lord Wenham's estate in Oxfordshire. He told her he had not a single farthing, but that if she would like to be Duchess of Clarence, and, perhaps, Queen of England, he should be happy to convey the honours to her. Report says, she accepted. On its being told to the Regent, His Royal Highness groaned—which is, it seems, his way of disapproving." There certainly was something in this. " There is a great commotion in the royal family, and with some reason," Sir William Henry Fremantle wrote to the Duke of Buckingham. " The Duke of Clarence has thought fit to propose to Miss Wykeham, who has accepted him. The Prince, accompanied by the Duchess of Gloucester, went to Windsor on Tuesday to inform the Queen of the happy event, who was, of course, outrageous. The Council have sat twice upon the business, and it is determined, as I understand, to oppose it." In the end, the engagement was broken off. In 1817, his Royal Highness offered himself to the Princess of Denmark, who would have none of him; but in the following year the Duke came to roost with Adelaide, the eldest daughter of the Duke of Saxe-Meiningen. There were two daughters of the marriage, but both died in infancy.

Mrs. Jordan had borne the Duke of Clarence ten children:

George, who went into the army;

Frederick, who became a Colonel, and married Lady Augusta, daughter of George Boyle, Earl of Glasgow;

Adolphus, who entered the navy;

Augustus, who took Holy Orders;

Henry, who died a Captain in India;

Sophia, who married Philip, eldest son of Sir Philip Sidney, Bart., of Penshurst Place, Kent;

Mary, who married Colonel (afterwards General) Fox, of the Grenadier Guards;

Elizabeth, who married William George, Earl of Errol, Hereditary Lord High Constable of Scotland,—one of the daughters, Lady Agnes, became the wife of Lord Fife, father of Edward VII's son-in-law;

Augusta, who married John Kennedy Erskine, second son of the Marquis of Ailsa; and

Amelia, who married Lucius Cary, Viscount Falkland.

When the Duke of Clarence came to the throne, one of the first things he did was to provide for his children by Dorothy Jordan. He created the eldest son, Earl of Munster, and to the rest he gave rank and precedency of sons and daughters of a marquis. In so doing, he followed, more or less closely, the example set by his predecessors, and people generally approved of his thus publicly recognising his offspring. Besides titles, he gave them large pensions secured on the Civil List, and appointed them to well-endowed sinecures. One son was made Governor of Windsor Castle for life at a salary of twelve hundred pounds a year; another was given the comfortable post of Governor of the Tower. For Lord Augustus Fitz-Clarence, who had taken Orders, was the fat rectory of Mapledurham, and a Canonry of Windsor; Lord Adolphus was a captain of the royal yacht. Lady Mary Fox became Housekeeper of Windsor Castle, and her sister Housekeeper of Kensington Palace. Lord Errol, who had married Lady Elizabeth Fitz-Clarence, was made Ranger of Windsor Park, and was given Pembroke Lodge for a residence. Queen Adelaide was very kind to the FitzClarences and had them constantly about her. She ranked the Fitz-Clarence Lords and Ladies as morganatic sons and daughters of the King. As such, she took Amelia to Germany, and brought her out at the Courts of Stuttgart and Saxe-Meiningen.

Queen Victoria, however, on her accession, finding herself so surrounded by FitzClarences, desired, perhaps not unnaturally, to remove some of them from their posts, and only refrained from doing so when it was pointed out to her that, should she do so, as the places had been given for life, they would have to be handsomely compensated.

William IV ordered Chantrey to execute a bust of Mrs. Jordan, to be set up in Westminster Abbey, with the inscription, " To Dora Bland, by one who loved her." The commission was executed, but the bust was not set up in the Abbey. " I met yesterday at dinner, at Sir William Dundas's, Sir Francis Chantrey, the sculptor, with whom I had a great deal of curious conversation about his intercourse with William IV," Mary Berry relates in her Journal. " Very soon after his accession to the throne, he sent for Chantrey, and told him he had a commission to give him that was very interesting to him. He was anxious to erect a monument to Mrs. Jordan, and desired the sculptor's opinion what it should be, and where it should be placed. To the latter enquiry he had no answer to give. The King then went into a thousand particulars of their private life, always ending that she had been an excellent mother to her children. He said he knew he had been much blamed for his conduct to her ; but that from the time they parted, he had allowed two thousand pounds a year, which was regularly paid every quarter, although often with great difficulty to himself to find the money. The monument Chantrey executed, and was paid for, but it remains still in his studio, where it is to be erected never having been settled during the King's life, and Lord Munster (the eldest of the children) having made some objection to where it was proposed to be placed."

IV

Shortly after the separation with the Duke of
Clarence in 1811 Mrs. Jordan returned to the stage.
She made her reappearance at Covent Garden on
July 11 as the Widow Cheerby. Her last performance at that theatre was on June 1, 1814, when she
played Lady Teazle. She took an informal farewell
of the stage at a brief season at Margate in August,
1815. Although her figure was matronly, and although,
in spite of this, she insisted on appearing in the parts
in which she had made her earlier triumphs, she was
to the end of her career as popular as ever with the
public in London and the provinces.

Mrs. Jordan's last years were clouded with unhappi-
ness, and over her hung the spectre of possible im-
prisonment for debt. Alsop, her eldest daughter's
husband, unquestionably robbed her, and had to be
got out of the country. She did what she could for
him, always, in spite of his shameful betrayal of her,
retaining some liking for him. He left his wife,
Frances, entirely destitute, and dependent on the
mother he had nearly beggared. Then, her two sons,
Captain George and Lieutenant Henry FitzClarence,
of the 10th Royal Hussars, were, with many other
officers, removed from that regiment for concurring
in that censure of their commanding officer, Colonel
George Quentin, which produced his court-martial in
October, 1814.

DOROTHY JORDAN
After a portrait by Romney

All this is revealed in a series of letters from Mrs. Jordan to a friend :—

" WHITEHAVEN, *November* 11, 1814.

" MY DEAR ——,

" This moment only have I received both your letters ; therefore, you will not be surprised that I grew uneasy. The other half of the cheque you will have received by this time. It was from Howard's own mouth that I got the disagreeable information, that I was liable to pay the additional insurance on Alsop's life. I need not tell you how much obliged I should be to you, if you would regularly arrange this very disagreeable and unfortunate business for me. I trust that the heavy addition will be *prevented*, and I am truly sorry that you have not been comfortable. What has been the matter ?

" I have been very ill, but do not let them know of it at home—so much so, that I was obliged to give up my engagement at Sheffield, after playing only one night, which was doubly unlucky from the prospect there was of great success. I am doing very well here, but the theatre is not large enough.

" God bless you all !

" Your affectionate

" D. J.

" I believe I shall go to Edinburgh—but Newcastle first."

" CARLISLE, *Saturday, December* 3, 1814.

" MY DEAR ——,

" I was prevented by illness both of body and mind the last time I wrote, from saying one-half of what it is necessary should be now perfectly understood with regard to Mrs. Alsop.

" You say that in order to assist her, you must expend £30 or £40. I am sorry for it, and it will not be in my power to reimburse you ; and trust the love and duty you owe to your own family will interfere, and point out to you the injustice of it. You talk of Mrs. Alsop's *desire* to go to her husband. If it were affection or duty that prompted her, I should pity, though, even in that case, it would at this time be out of my power to forward her wishes ; but *this* is not the case, as you *know*. I have at present melancholy, but far better, claims on me—claims that, to my bitter remorse, I have almost deprived myself of the means of affording to two amiable children, by having lavished them on one. She could never have been sensible of the sacrifice, or I should not have met with such *ingratitude*.

" For the last time shall this subject ever employ my pen, and I trust you will give it the attention I feel due to it. In the event of Mrs. Alsop's going abroad, I must sink another £100 per year to the £260 (independent of the additional insurance on Alsop's life), making in all near £400 a year. He has no employment, and how will he support her ? and am I to have the *additional* misery of thinking she may be *starving* in a *foreign* land ? I, therefore, for the *last time*, most solemnly declare to her, through you, that these are the last and only propositions that shall ever be offered. THAT she shall go to her uncle in Wales, when I will pay £40 a year for her board and lodging, allowing her £50 a year for clothes, till such time her husband may be able to maintain her abroad, when every exertion shall be made to send her out. If she refuses this, I here *swear* by the most heart-breaking oath that presents itself to my tortured mind, that, ' may I never again see *those two sacrificed young men* [her sons, George and Henry FitzClarence], if I ever (if possible) think of her again as a child that has any claim on me.' And I shall be led to doubt the affection of any one who may, by a mistaken motive, endeavour to make me break an oath so seriously and solemnly taken. If she has an atom of feeling, and wishes to regain any part of my affection, she will *instantly* agree to this : if *not*, the £90 a year shall be regularly paid to her so long as I have it to give. Let her not look on this as a *banishment :* let her look on the fate of two gallant young men, submitting to a cruel exile without a *murmur*, whatever they may feel.

" I shall send a plan to Mrs. Williams, and shall be under the disagreeable necessity of withdrawing from you the little addition I could have wished to continue to you. When everything is adjusted, it will be impossible for me to remain in England. I shall, therefore, go *abroad*, appropriating as much as I can spare

R

of the remainder of my income to pay my debts.
And now for the last time on this cruel subject, *adieu.*
I write this from a sleepless pillow. God bless you
all! I shall be home by the 15th or 16th. I have
been obliged to give up all my engagements. Love
to all.

" Your affectionate,

" D. J.

" For the little while I shall be in Cadogan Place,
after the departure of all happiness. Tell dear Lucy
that I will pay her three guineas a week, for myself,
Miss S[ketchley], and the two servants, finding our
own tea, sugar, and wine. Be silent on the subject of my going *abroad,* or it may *embarrass*
me."

" CARLISLE, Sunday, December 4, 1814.

" MY DEAR ——,

" When I received your letter relative to
Fanny [*i.e.,* Frances Alsop], I wrote immediately to
George [FitzClarence], without endeavouring to prejudice him in the smallest degree—but was not at all
surprised at the enclosed answer, which you may
show or not, as you shall judge best. You have, of
course, received my last. I will spare what I can to
send her to Wales respectable, and enable her uncle
to receive her comfortably. Whenever Alsop is
in a situation to provide for, or maintain her
abroad, I will exert my utmost to send her to
him.

" All personal discussions on such subjects are doubly painful ; therefore, to prevent such, I take the opportunity of repeating this by letter ; and, in future, I have only to refer Fanny to my last letter to you. If she and Mrs. Williams should prefer living in any cheap part of France, they may do it to more advantage. It is very probable I shall find it necessary to live there the best part of every year. Dear George's account of everybody in C. Place gives me great pleasure. I could wish Mrs. Alsop and Mrs. Williams would make up their minds before I return. I shall be back, if those dear boys go soon, by the 15th or 16th. God bless you all !

" Your affectionate

" D. J."

Enclosure.

Captain George FitzClarence to Dorothy Jordan.

" London, *December* 2, 1814.

" My dearest Mother,

" Nothing is as yet settled when we start ; but we are to go out in Admiral Burlton's ship, who goes out to take the command in India. I am now certain to join Lord Moira ; but, if anything is said about it, the Duke of York will give me positive orders to join my horrid regiment. I really think we go out in the most happy way, and *ought*, if we choose to stay long enough, to make our fortunes. My father, poor soul, has suffered much, but is now better ; his anxiety actually made him very ill—but both go out

in the same ship, which is a great comfort. Although
we are a great way off each other (700 miles), yet I
hope, should any good situation offer, to bring Henry
to Calcutta. The girls have made up their minds to
it very well. M—— did not mention anything about
Fanny ; but I cannot take her on board the King's
ship. It will be impossible ; I would not shackle
myself with her. MacMahon gives me the most *certain
assurances* of Alsop being provided for. I will do all
I can ; but I cannot take Fanny out with us. It
will cost £3000 to get us out to India—where is all
this to come from ? "

"CARLISLE, *December* 5, 1814.

" MY DEAR ——,

"I shall be home by January 15th or 16th.
Truly sorry am I to be under the necessity of disturb-
ing Dora ; sooner than do so, if I were not very
unwell, I would take lodgings.

"The enclosed to the General [Hawker, her son-in-
law] contains a proposition, similar to the one I made
to you, concerning the house ; which, if it does not
appear eligible to him, I shall dispose of as soon as
possible—and, if I am not able to follow my profession, I shall immediately go abroad. God bless
you !

"D. J.

"I trust in God you will exert yourself in
pointing out to Fanny the *absolute necessity* of

her prompt compliance with the proposal; in which case, she shall ever find me her mother and friend."

Mrs. Jordan, accompanied by a Miss Sketchley, fled to France late in 1815, and stayed at Boulogne, hiding her identity under the style of Mrs. James, and taking the further precaution of having her letters addressed to the post office. Her old friend could not understand the reason for her flight, though he was conversant with her affairs. " The malicious representations of her having been left straightened in pecuniary circumstances were literally *fabulous*; for to the very moment of her death, she remained in full possession of all the means of comfort—nay, if she chose it, of *luxury* and *splendour*," he writes. " Why, therefore, she emigrated, pined away, and expired in a foreign country (of whose language she was ignorant, and in whose habits she was wholly unversed), with every appearance of necessity, is also considered a mystery by those unacquainted with the cruel and disastrous circumstances which caused that unfortunate catastrophe. It is not by my pen that miserable story shall be told. It was a transaction wherein her royal friend had *directly* or *indirectly* no concern; nor did it in any way spring out of that connection. She had, in fact, only to accuse herself of benevolence, confidence, and honour, to those demerits, and to the worse than ingratitude of others, she fell a lingering, broken-hearted victim."

It was unquestionable financial trouble that made Mrs. Jordan leave England. The details of her troubles are not quite clear, but such statements as have been published shall be given.

An Authentic Statement.

" In the autumn of 1813, Mrs. Jordan was called upon very unexpectedly, to redeem some securities given by her, for money raised to assist a near relative. The cause of this aid was the pressure of matters, purely of a domestic nature. The call upon her was sudden, and certainly unexpected; and, not finding herself in a situation to advance the £2000 claimed, she withdrew herself to France, deputing a friend in England to make every necessary arrangement for paying all her creditors as soon as possible. At the time of Mrs. Jordan's quitting England, she was in the receipt of an annual income of upwards of £2000 paid with the greatest punctuality quarterly, without demur, drawback, or impediment, and so continued to the hour of her death."—[This was her share of the settlement made on behalf of the Duke of Clarence]—" Up to April 16, Mrs. Jordan's drafts on Messrs. Coutts & Co. were duly paid; never for a moment could she have felt the gripping hand of poverty.

" I can positively assert, that never during her lifetime was one shilling paid towards *liquidating* the securities in question; nor was it urgent that it should be done : because the creditors, for the most part personal friends, well knew the upright principles they had to depend upon ; nor were they ignorant, that the transcendent talents of this gifted being were always sure to receive a munificent reward from the hands of the public, whenever she should again seek their assistance ; and in the fruits of this, they were sure of participating. Her protracted stay abroad was occasioned by untoward circumstances, over which the principals had no control.

" Up to the hour of Mrs. Jordan's leaving England, she had been living under the same roof with the relative with whom she was concerned in the securities alluded to. Reciprocal acts of kindness, mutual confidence, in all domestic affairs, and many points of private affairs, tended to create in Mrs. Jordan's mind a reliance upon this person. Never for a moment during the six years that her daughter had been married, had Mrs. Jordan reason to doubt his sincere affection or his veracity ; nor did she doubt them when she left England.

" Immediately upon the derangement of Mrs. Jordan's affairs, and *before* she left England, a statement of all the claims to which she was liable was made out, together with a list of the persons holding her bonds and bills of acceptance ; the result of which convinced Mrs. Jordan that her liabilities did not much exceed £2000, and that the claimants were one and all the personal friends of the parties.

" In August, 1815, Mrs. Jordan left England for France, with the intention of remaining away some

ten days, the time computed necessary to place matters
in that state, as to render her person legally secure
from arrest. Her affairs were placed in the hands of
persons well informed in every particular thereof, as
of all other matters connected with her life. Mrs.
Jordan was well aware that the creditors were only
anxious to have their claims placed in a secure state,
and that they were willing to give every accommoda-
tion required. She was also aware that her fellow-
sufferer had given up a considerable portion of his
income ; and she felt that her representative in
England could in one hour's time settle any doubtful
point that might arise during the arrangement. In
short, she knew that no impediment existed. Consequently, when she found that month after month
elapsed, without anything being finally settled, her
mind became troubled.

" Mrs. Jordan left England ; she took with her as
a companion a lady [Miss Sketchley] who had for some
years previously been employed in superintending the
education of Mrs. Jordan's younger children, and who
had, for the last twelve months, been Mrs. Jordan's
constant companion. This person came to England
in January 1816, to receive and take Mrs. Jordan her
quarter's income, then in Messrs. Coutts' house.
From the moment of her arrival in England, until she
quitted it, she pursued a line of conduct towards the
daughters of Mrs. Jordan (then residing in Mrs.
Jordan's house) that was offensive beyond measure.
She peremptorily, and in a most insulting manner,
called upon the person concerned with Mrs. Jordan

in the affair of the bills and bonds, to make oath that
Mrs. Jordan was not liable to any claims *beyond* those
of which she already knew. The demand was accompanied by base insinuations. Justly doubting this to
be really the work of Mrs. Jordan, and irritated at the
circumstances at ending the demand, it was *refused*;
and, on the same day, this lady returned to
France, and, there is little doubt but then, for
the first time, Mrs. Jordan did become 'apprehen-
sive.'

"During her stay in England, the lady alluded to
informed two of Mrs. Jordan's daughters, that Mrs.
Jordan's future place of residence in France was to
be kept a profound secret from them, and that all
letters from them to their mother must be sent through
a third person, and directed to Mrs. James, instead
of Mrs. Jordan; thus, from that time, all such com-
munications first passed through the hands of a person
who might withdraw Mrs. Jordan's confidence and
affection from those most interested in getting her
back to England. It is necessary to revert to the
verbal refusal given to take the oath demanded,
because it has been made a point of much importance
as connected with Mrs. Jordan's state of feeling,
in consequence of the publication made in the
Morning Chronicle of January 26, 1824, of a
letter of Mrs. Jordan's, bearing date, January 16,
1816.

"Mrs. Jordan's letter must have been written immediately after the return of the above-mentioned
lady to France, and there is great reason to think that

then *only*, for the first time, did a feeling of apprehension of further demands awake in Mrs. Jordan's mind, and the fatal step of cutting off the source of communication prevented altogether, or perhaps only delayed, the receipt of a letter, written by the person refusing to take the oath, on *the very same day*, to say that he was truly willing to do whatever Mrs. Jordan should *herself* require, and that the oath should be taken whenever she wrote to say it was *her wish.*

" There can be no question that the mind of this great woman had been long and grievously oppressed —nor will this be any matter of wonder when a retrospect is taken of her eventful life. Who can deny that, in the greatest flow of her prosperity, she had many bitter memorials that good and ill will mingle in every human condition ? The greatest pleasure that acquiring wealth could bestow on Mrs. Jordan, was its power of shedding greater happiness around her. Can there be a severer censure on her memory, than to think that pecuniary difficulties, even *weighty* (which hers never were), could for any length of time have depressed a mind, such as hers, in its perfect state ? "

As Mrs. Jordan died intestate, the King's Solicitor, *ex officio*, collected her effects. Accordingly letters of administration were taken out by the Solicitors to the Treasury on May 24, 1817 ; and the property was sworn to be under £300. It was not until 1824, however, that the estate was distributed, when her creditors received five shillings in the pound. Of course, aspersions were made upon the Duke of Clarence, and it was said that he had left her to die in poverty abroad. The whole circumstances were set forth for what was in fact, though not formally, an official statement by John Barton, of the Royal Mint, which was circulated to the Press :

" *January* 21, 1824.

" The attention of the public has lately, as it has many times before, been drawn, by notices in the daily papers, to the case of the late Mrs. Jordan, and much pains have been taken to stigmatise the conduct of an illustrious personage, as it relates to that cele- brated and much esteemed favourite of the public. These censures on the conduct of the Duke of Clarence have been often repeated, and as often treated with silence upon the part of his Royal Highness's friends. This silence, however, has been construed by many into an admission of the accusations ; till, at length, the stories so often told, of Mrs. Jordan's having been obliged to leave her country and fly to a neighbouring kingdom, where, it is said, she died insolvent, for want of a trifling allowance being made to her by the Duke, are assumed as facts.

" It has gone on thus until some persons have exclaimed, ' Has the Duke of Clarence no friend, who, if the accusations are groundless, can rescue the char- acter of his Royal Highness from such gross calumny ? ' All who know the Duke, or his connections, intimately, are acquainted with the truth ; but none being so

fully possessed of the whole case as myself, I feel that
any further forbearance would amount to a derelic-
tion of duty on my part, and, therefore, in justice to
a much-injured character, I take upon myself to
submit the following statement to the public, acquainting them, in the first place, that it was through my
hands the whole transaction upon the separation of
the Duke and Mrs. Jordan passed ; that it was at my
suggestion Mrs. Jordan adopted the resolution of
leaving this country for France, to enable her the more
readily and honourably to extricate herself from the
troubles into which she had fallen through a mis-
placed confidence, and that I possess a correspondence
with Mrs. Jordan, subsequent to her leaving England,
which corroborates my statement in the minutest
points.

" Upon the separation which took place between
Mrs. Jordan and the Duke, in the year 1811, it was
agreed that she should have the care, until a certain
age, of her four youngest daughters, and a settlement
was made by the Duke for the payment by him of
the following amounts :—

For the maintenance of his four daughters .   . £1,500
For a house and carriage for their use   .   . 600
For Mrs. Jordan's own use   1,500
And to enable Mrs. Jordan to make a provision for
    her married daughters, children of a former
    connection 800

in all   £4,400

" This settlement was carried into effect, a trustee

was appointed, and the monies, under such trust, were paid quarterly to the respective accounts at the banking-house of Messrs. Coutts & Co.

" It was a stipulation in the said settlements, that in the event of Mrs. Jordan resuming her profession, the care of the Duke's four daughters, together with the £1500 *per annum* for their maintenance, should revert to his Royal Highness ; and this event actually did take place in the course of a few months, in consequence of Mrs. Jordan's desire to accept certain proposals made to her to perform.   Mrs. Jordan did resume her profession ; and, not long after, reflections were thrown out against both the Duke and herself ; whereupon, Mrs. Jordan, indignant at such an attack upon his Royal Highness, wrote the following letter, which was published in the papers of the day :

" ' SIR,

" ' Though I did not see the morning print that contained the paragraph alluded to in your liberal and respectable paper of yesterday, yet I was not long left in ignorance of the abuse it poured out against me.   This I could silently have submitted to ; but I was by no means aware that the writer of it had taken the opportunity of throwing out insinuations which he thought might be injurious to a no less honourable than illustrious personage.

" ' In the love of truth, and in justice to his Royal Highness, I think it my duty, publicly and unequivocally, to declare that his liberality towards me has been noble and generous in the *highest degree ;* but, not having it in his power to extend his bounty beyond the term of his own existence, he has, with his accustomed goodness and consideration, allowed me to endeavour to make that provision for myself, which an event, that better feelings than those of *interest,* make me hope I shall never live to see, would entirely deprive me of.

"'This, then, sir, is my motive for returning to my profession. I am too happy in having every reason to hope and believe, that, under these circumstances, I shall not offend the public at large by seeking their *support* and *protection ;* and while I feel that I possess those, I shall patiently submit to that species of unmanly persecution, which a female so particularly situated must always be subject to. Ever ready to acknowledge my deficiencies in every respect, I trust I may add, that I shall never be found wanting in candour and gratitude—not forgetful of the care that every individual should feel for the good opinion of the public.

"'I am, Sir,

"'Your much obliged, humble servant,

"'DORA JORDAN.'"

"It should have been before stated, that upon settling the annual allowance to Mrs. Jordan, everything in the shape of a money transaction was brought to account ; and that the most trifling sums even, upon recollection, were admitted ; and interest being calculated upon the whole, in her favour, to the latest period, the balance was paid over to me, on the part of the Duke, and for which I hold Mrs. Jordan's receipt. It should also be understood that up to the day of their separation, Mrs. Jordan had received a large annual allowance from his Royal Highness.

" A cessation of correspondence between Mrs. Jordan and myself ensued until September, 1815, when I most unexpectedly received a note from her, requesting to see me immediately. I found her in tears, and under much embarrassment, from a circumstance that had burst upon her, as she said, ' like a thunder storm.' She found herself involved to a considerable amount by securities, which all at once appeared against her, in the forms of bonds and promissory notes, given incautiously by herself, to relieve, as she thought, from trifling difficulties, *a near relation, in whom she had placed the greatest confidence.*

" Acceptances had been given by her in *blank*, upon stamped paper, which she supposed were for small amounts ; but which afterwards appear to have been laid before her capable of carrying larger sums.

" She was fearful of immediate arrest. She wished to treat all her claimants most fairly and honourably, and to save, if possible, the wife and children of the person who had so deceived her, from utter ruin. She could not enter into negotiations with her creditors, unless at large ; and, apprehending that, if she remained in England, that would not long be the case, she instantly adopted the resolution before mentioned, of going to France.

" A list of creditors was made out, and an arrangement was in progress to enable her to return to this country. All she required, in order to set her mind at ease on the extent of the demands that might be out against her was, that the person who had plunged her into all these difficulties should declare, upon oath, that the list he had given to her included the whole. This the party from time to time refused to do ; and disappointed thus in the hope she had so fondly cherished, of again returning to this country, and seeing those children for whom she had the most tender affection, she sunk under the weight of her afflictions, and in the month of July 1816 died at St. Cloud.

" In support of the foregoing narrative, the writer has the most incontestable evidence ; but he trusts nothing can be more satisfactory or convincing to the public, than the following extract from a letter addressed by Mrs. Jordan to him, dated at Paris, January 18, 1816.

" ' DEAR SIR,

" ' I have forborn writing to you, that I might occupy as little of your time as possible. My spirits are in so disturbed a state, that my weak hand is scarcely able to trace the still more feeble efforts of my mind. . . . He assures you that I am in possession of the names of my creditors, to whom he has made me answerable, by filling up those blank acceptances that I so unguardedly gave him ; and *yet declines* making an oath to that *purpose :* this has caused me much uneasiness, for it appears to me *vague,* if not *equivocal.*

" ' I can solemnly declare that the names I sent to you, are the only ones I know, and the greater part utter strangers to me.

" ' I was in hopes that, not only out of humanity and justice to me, but for his own sake, he would have done it voluntarily, as it would have been the means of removing, in a great degree, the unpleasant impressions such a determination might cause in the minds of those who still remain anxious for the future well-doing. I do not command or enforce it, but *entreat* it as the only relief he can give to a being he has almost destroyed. . . . What interpretation can be put on his refusal ? If he says he will not take the oath, it is *cruel,* and if he add that he *cannot,* what is to become of me ? Is it in human nature possible for me to return to an uncertain home, with all the horrors I have suffered there fresh on my mind ; with the constant dread of what may be hurrying after me ? I really think (under those circumstances), that when my presence would be absolutely necessary, that it would not remain *in my own power* to be able to encounter such misery. It is not, believe me, the feelings of *pride, avarice,* or the absence of *those comforts* I have all my life been accustomed to, that is killing me by inches ; it is the loss of my only remaining comfort, *the hope I used to live on, from time to*

s

time of seeing my children. The above assertion I can convince the world of, if driven to it, by leaving the bond (all I have) to the creditors, and the Duke's generous allowance, to the decision of the law.

" ' It is now, and ever has been, my wish to save ——— ; for, even now, I feel a regard for him I cannot conquer ; but surely I may expect some return of gratitude from a man, who, by a single act, could relieve those fears that are nearly *insupportable.* The idea is shocking.

" ' Excuse this long letter ; but I am sure you will see and feel the motives and the urgency. Once more, dear sir, forgive and excuse,

" Yours,

" ' DORA JORDAN.'

" With the death of Mrs. Jordan ceased the allowance which, by his Royal Highness's means, she was enabled to make up £200 a year, to each of her three married daughters. Surely, then, no blame can attach to the Duke of Clarence, whose liberality, in order to enable Mrs. Jordan to make a suitable provision for them, in the event of her death, has been acknowledged by her to have been ' most noble and generous in the highest degree.'

" All sorts of means were resorted to by one of the parties (now no more) to *compel* a continuance of these allowances. The Duke did not choose to be driven in this respect ; but when the importunity, from inefficacy of threats, had died away, his Royal Highness, of his own generous accord, did give to each his kind assistance, and I am, to this day, paying, and, as long as it shall be his Royal Highness's pleasure, shall continue to pay, annual gratuities to the two surviving daughters.

"Who, then, after this statement of *facts*, shall accuse the Duke of Clarence with want of generosity towards Mrs. Jordan or her memory?

"The administration of the effects of Mrs. Jordan by the Solicitors of the Treasury was *ex officio;* and the advertisement[1] which appeared in the papers, and which has called forth this last attack, was put in, in regular discharge of the duties of his administration.

"I must conclude with one assurance, that after having given a true, and, I trust, a candid recital of fact, I shall treat with contempt anything further that may be said on the subject; resting satisfied if, after an attachment of six-and-thirty years' service to a good and generous master, I shall have added anything to his comfort in convincing a single individual of the injustice he has sustained."

[1] "DOROTHEA JORDAN, DECEASED.—The creditors of Dorothea Jordan, late of Englefield Green, and Cadogan Place, Sloane Street, in the County of Middlesex, spinster, deceased, who have proved their debts, may receive a dividend of five shillings in the pound, by applying at the office of the Solicitor to the Treasury, No. 5, Stone Buildings, Lincoln's Inn. And those creditors who have not yet proved their debts, are requested forthwith to present the Solicitor to the Treasury with proof thereof."

Mrs. Jordan was at Paris later in the year, and there received the following letter from one of her sons :

Colonel Frederick FitzClarence to Dorothy Jordan.

" [PARIS, 1815].

" MY DEAR MOTHER,

"My dear [sister] Sophia has been very low-spirited ever since she received my ever-dear Dora [March]'s letter; and she took the earliest opportunity to speak to Mrs. Arbuthnot, who would speak to her husband about it. I am afraid we shall not come home for this long time. I long to see dear Lucy [Hawker]. The Arbuthnots are very kind to me. I have got a room in Paris. I have had a horse shot. Tell me about the ——'s. If you want money for them, don't ask me for it, but take *my* allowance for them ; because, with a little care, I could live on my father's, till *their* business is settled. Now do as I ask you—mind you do ; for they have always been so kind to us all : and, if I can make any return, I should be a devil if I did not ; so take my next quarter—and, as you may want to give them some, do that for *my sake*. I am very well. God bless you !

" FRED. FITZCLARENCE.

" Sophia will write to you on Thursday."

Mrs. Jordan went from Paris to St. Cloud.   Sir

Jonah Barrington says she suffered from jaundice, called by the French *la maladie noire*. She ought to have taken exercise, but she rarely rose from her couch. She ought to have seen company, but she was solitary. She ought to have been in cheerful surroundings—yet this is the description of her last home : " The apartments she occupied at St. Cloud were in a house in a square adjoining the Palace. The house was large, gloomy, cold, and inconvenient, just the sort of place which would tell in description in romance. In fact, it looked to me almost in a state of dilapidation. I could not, I am sure, wander over it at night without a superstitious feeling. The rooms were numerous, but small ; the furniture scanty, old, and tattered. The hotel had obviously once belonged to some nobleman, and a long, lofty, flagged gallery stretched from one wing of it to the other. Mrs. Jordan's chambers were shabby : no English comforts solaced her in her latter moments ! In her little drawing-room, a small old sofa was the best-looking piece of furniture. On this, she constantly reclined, and on this she died. The garden in her time was over-grown with weeds, and two melancholy cypress trees pointed, and almost confined her reflections, to the grave." Her troubles were serious, but not by any means irremediable. She was only fifty-three years of age, with at least a decade of successful and profitable work on the stage ; but this mother of fifteen children, to each and all of whom she was devoted, was no doubt, in spite of her amazing vitality, a tired woman. The separation from her royal lover of a score of years utterly shattered her, and she was too weary to rebuild her life. Then came the crowning blow of Alsop's infamy. Mrs. Jordan's one desire at St. Cloud was for letters from home. On the morning of her death, C——, the owner of the house in which she lived, told Sir Jonah Barrington, " the agitation was almost fearful : her eyes were now restless, now fixed ; her motion rapid and unmeaning ; and her whole manner seemed to bespeak the attack of some convulsive paroxysm." He went for her to the post office ; and on his return she held out her hand for letters, but there were none. " She stood for a moment motionless ; looked towards him with a vacant stare ; held out her hand again, as if by an involuntary action ; instantly withdrew it, and sank back upon the sofa from which she had arisen. Mr. C—— now left the room to send up her attendant, but she had gone out. He, therefore, returned to Mrs. Jordan. On approaching her, he observed some change in her looks that alarmed him. She spoke not a word, but gazed at him steadfastly. She wept not—no tear flowed. Her face was one moment flushed, another livid. She sighed deeply, and her heart seemed bursting. Mr. C—— stood, uncertain what to do ; but in a minute he heard her breath drawn more hardly, and, as it were, sobbingly. He was now thoroughly terrified ; he hastily approached the sofa, and leaning over the unfortunate lady, discovered that those deep-drawn sobs had immediately preceded the moment of Mrs. Jordan's dissolution. She was already no more."

Mrs. Jordan died on July 3, 1816, in her fifty-fourth year. She was buried in the cemetery of St. Cloud, the ceremony being performed by Mr. Forster, the Chaplain to the British Embassy at Paris.

INDEX

281